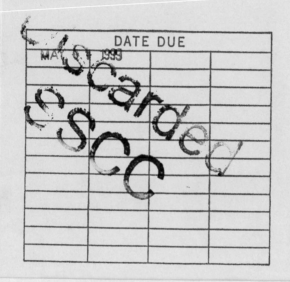

Science and the
National Environmental
Policy Act

Science
and the
National
Environmental
Policy Act

Redirecting Policy through Procedural Reform

LYNTON K. CALDWELL

The University of Alabama Press

Library of Congress Cataloging in Publication Data

Caldwell, Lynton Keith, 1913–
    Science and the National Environmental Policy
Act.

    Lectures presented at the University of Alabama
in March 1981 under the auspices of the Center for
Administrative Policy Studies.
    Bibliography: p.
    Includes index.
    1. Environmental impact analysis—United States.
2. Environmental law—United States. I. United
States. National Environmental Policy Act of 1969.
II. University of Alabama. Center for Administrative and Policy Studies. III. Title.

TD194.6.C34   353.07'2   81-21884
ISBN 0-8173-0111-9   AACR2
ISBN 0-8173-0112-7 (pbk.)

Contents

Preface

This book was prepared originally as a series of lectures presented at The University of Alabama in the spring of 1981. These lectures are part of a longer series in public policy and administration that since 1945 has been widely known as The Alabama Lectures. Over the years this series has highlighted important developments in the management of political affairs. The lectures have summarized and anticipated many critical trends in public administration. These chapters, expanded somewhat from my 1981 lectures, continue that tradition.

When John M. Gaus, then of the University of Wisconsin, delivered one of the first of the series in late November of 1945, some thirty-five years ago, his first topic was the ecology of government. Ecology was then a word that most people needed to look up in a dictionary. "An ecological approach to public administration," declared Gaus, "builds...quite literally from the ground up; from the elements of a place—soils, climate, location, for example—to the people who live there—their names and ages and knowledge, and the ways of physical and social technology by which from the place and in relationship with one another, they get their living."*

We are now no less concerned with the ecology of government, but a new dimension has been added to the Gausian

---

*John Morrison Gaus, *Reflections on Public Administration* (University, Ala.: University of Alabama Press, 1947), pp. 8–9.

perspective—that of ecology and government. Troubles have arisen in the people-environment relationships that were the focus of Gaus's concern. Ecology as a rapidly maturing science has become an instrument of national policy and, in a way that Gaus could not have foreseen, has become, through the National Environmental Policy Act, a force for the reformation of public administration. In his first Alabama lecture, Gaus spoke of "the importance of social institutions or devices," and I believe that he would have taken a profound interest in the invention of the environmental impact statement as an action-forcing mechanism to induce an ecological conscience in the conduct of public administration.

In a sense, therefore, this book represents a full circle from the first Alabama lectures. We are now able to consider how the philosophical approach of John Gaus to the understanding of public administration has become institutionalized in an innovative public law of the United States.

The subject of the 1981 lectures is also timely because responsibility for a project to improve the content and methodology of environmental impact analysis, funded by the National Science Foundation, had recently caused me to consider carefully the relationship of impact analysis to the National Environmental Policy Act and its objectives. As a participant in the drafting of the act, I was familiar with its history and the intended use of the impact statement required under Section 102(2)(c). But I had never had occasion to consider at length the distinctive strategy embodied in the act to use an administrative procedure as a vehicle for applying an integrated interdisciplinary use of science to achieve a redirection of national policy.

Although the National Science Foundation project on the uses of science in environmental impact statements provided an occasion and a stimulus for choosing the topic of the 1981 lectures, it was collateral to and only indirectly contributory to them. Nearly all of the data for the NSF project were collected after the lectures were prepared; therefore, material presented here from interviews with scientists and administrators was gathered after the lectures were given. The thought and analysis that went into the preparation of this book helped significantly to refine the issues examined in the NSF project. There was, therefore, a linkage between these separate efforts that benefited each.

Acknowledgments are owed to the following persons who made this volume possible: at The University of Alabama, Coleman B. Ransom, Jr., professor, and Philip B. Coulter, chairman of the Department of Political Science, at whose invitation the lectures leading to this book were given, and Malcolm M. MacDonald, whose interest and receptivity led to publication.

In the preparation and editing of this manuscript, I owe a particular debt of appreciation and gratitude to Robert V. Bartlett of the Department of Political Science at Indiana University. His critical judgment and informed review throughout all stages of the writing of this book contributed greatly to whatever quality the final product may possess. Richard Carpenter of the East-West Center Environment and Policy Institute, Bruce Bandurski of the Bureau of Land Management, and David L. Keys of Indiana University gave helpful detailed comments. William Grange assisted with researching bibliographical and factual details. The processing of the manuscript in its several stages was competently performed by Susan Von Der Haar, Brenda Hagenmaier, Helene Ward, Doris Verkamp, and Linda DuPlantis. I wish also to thank Jan Lundy for general assistance and the many federal agency personnel whose observations brought the leaven of practical experience to theoretical perspectives.

Science and the
National Environmental
Policy Act

1
Implementing Policy
through Procedure

The purposes of this Act are: To declare a national policy which will encourage productive and enjoyable harmony between man and his environment; to promote efforts which will prevent or eliminate damage to the environment and biosphere and stimulate the health and welfare of man; to enrich the understanding of the ecological systems and natural resources important to the Nation; and to establish a Council on Environmental Quality.

This book describes how a procedural invention was enlisted to effect the major reorientation of public policy and administration required by the National Environmental Policy Act (NEPA) of 1969. The purpose of the procedure—environmental impact analysis—was to force federal officials to consider the possible consequences of decisions having major implications for the quality of the human environment. The National Environmental Policy Act was not meant to force any particular decision on an agency; it required the agency to certify through an environmental impact statement (EIS) that it had investigated and considered the environmental implications of its proposed actions. The EIS was intended to set forth the environmental facts relative to proposed public action. It was conceived as a mandatory, action-forcing reorientation of planning and decisionmaking. But it was never intended to preempt the decisionmaking authority of responsible public officials. It was intended to influence the way in which this decisionmaking authority was exercised.

To achieve environmental impact analysis, an effective policy-focused use of scientific knowledge and method was necessary, and it was to answer this need that the EIS was
conceived. Although not itself a scientific document, the EIS
depends for its usefulness upon the adequacy of its knowledge
base, which, given the questions the EIS addresses, must necessarily be sought in the sciences. But adequacy is conditioned
not only by the scope and quality of the science employed; it is
also determined by how this knowledge is deployed. To obtain a
policy-focused use of science in environmental impact analysis,
two instrumental reforms were required. The first was a reordering of assumptions regarding the relevance of scientific
knowledge and method to federal planning and decisionmaking. The second was a restructuring of administrative procedures to ensure that the implications of the reordered view of
science were considered in agency planning and decisionmaking, consistent with the purposes of the act.

Enlistment of science on behalf of policy was necessary because only through science, broadly defined, could the impact
of man's activities upon the environment adequately be assessed and remedial measures be applied where needed.
Achievement of the NEPA policy declaration required that
reliable analyses of environmental effects and relationships be
built into and guide the planning and decision processes of
government, but without predetermining final action. Such
analyses were to be derived from the sciences, but could not be
obtained through the ways governments had traditionally
used science. To achieve NEPA goals, an integrated interdisciplinary use of science was necessary to address complex
and interrelated environmental problems. Recognition of the
need to redeploy and reintegrate scientific knowledge to respond to the complex challenges of environmental policy gave
practical expression to the theoretical unity of science.

To obtain such integrative use of science, administrative
procedures had to be reformed. Administrative arrangements
were needed to ensure that planners and decisionmakers not
only took account of the environmental impact of their actions,
but that they obtained the information to enable them to carry

out their responsibilities as extended by NEPA. These included consideration of alternative means of accomplishing public purposes and of the environmental implications of such alternatives. Science therefore provided the substantive element in redirecting national policy for the environment through procedural reform. The critical procedure—the environmental impact statement—became the vector, carrying integrated interdisciplinary sciences into the shaping of public policy.

NEPA in Summary

The National Environmental Policy Act of 1969 committed the government of the United States for the first time in its history to a comprehensive policy of environmental protection. To understand the implications of NEPA on specific federal policies and procedures, an appreciation of its broad purpose is required. The act is reprinted in full in the Appendix.

Although brief in text, NEPA is comprehensive in substance. Title I declares a national policy for the environment, identifying six general goals toward achievement of which "it is the continuing responsibility of the Federal Government to use all practicable means, consistent with other essential considerations of national policy." A controversial provision in Section 101 originally stated that "the Congress recognizes that each person has a right to a healthful environment." Under 101(c) as enacted, this "right" was deleted and the phrase "should enjoy a healthful environment" substituted. The argument for this change was that the right to a healthful environment was without remedy—the provision would have been unenforceable. To have defined "a healthful environment" would have exceeded the capabilities of science (if not of politics) and raised a host of legal implications regarding the rights of persons compelled by circumstances to work under conditions potentially hazardous to health—for example, in association with persons smoking tobacco.

Section 102 is the administrative or procedural part of NEPA. In essence it is a set of instructions from the Congress to the federal agencies regarding their implementation of the purposes of the act through planning and decisionmaking. Science is made an integral part of the implementation process through Section 102(2), which reads unequivocally that all agencies of the federal government shall

(a) Utilize a systematic, interdisciplinary approach which will insure the integrated use of the natural and social sciences and the environmental design arts in planning and decisionmaking which may have an impact on man's environment;

(b) Identify and develop methods and procedures, in consultation with the Council on Environmental Quality...which will insure that presently unquantified environmental amenities and values may be given appropriate consideration in decisionmaking along with economic and technical considerations.

That these were not rhetorical admonitions is made evident in the opening lines of Section 102 and in Section 102(2)(c):

The Congress authorizes and directs that, to the fullest possible extent: (1) the policies, regulations, and public laws of the United States shall be interpreted and administered in accordance with the policies set forth in this Act, and (2) all agencies of the Federal Government shall—

(c) Include in every recommendation or report on proposals for legislation and other major Federal actions significantly affecting the quality of the human environment, a detailed statement by the responsible official on—

(i) The environmental impact of the proposed action,

(ii) Any adverse environmental effects which cannot be avoided should the proposal be implemented,

(iii) Alternatives to the proposed action,

(iv) The relationship between local short-term uses of man's environment and the maintenance and enhancement of long-term productivity, and

(v) Any irreversible and irretrievable commitments of resources which would be involved in the proposed action should it be implemented.

In addition, Section 102(e) requires the agencies to "study, develop, and describe appropriate alternatives to recommended courses of action in any proposal which involves unresolved conflicts concerning alternative uses of available resources" and (h) to "initiate and utilize ecological information in the planning and development of resource-oriented projects." Other sections of the act contain provisions important for particular issues, for example, those involving international cooperation. Two additional provisions affecting agency responsibility deserve mention. The first (Section 103) requires all agencies to review their statutory mandate to determine whether it contains deficiencies or inconsistencies that would prohibit full compliance with the act. The second (Section 105) declares the goals and policies set forth in NEPA to be "supplementary to those set forth in existing authorities of Federal agencies." Thus, in effect, NEPA amended all basic authorizing statutes to which its policies and procedures applied.

Title II of NEPA establishes the three-member Council on Environmental Quality (CEQ), specifies its powers, and provides that the president shall transmit to the Congress annually an environmental quality report. The contents of the report are specified in the statute (Section 201), and its preparation falls largely to the CEQ (Section 204).

Assessments of the significance and effectiveness of NEPA vary with the perspective of the viewers. Charles Ross, former member of the Federal Power Commission, found NEPA to be a sophisticated piece of legislation.[1] John B. Calhoun of the National Institute of Mental Health concurred with Russell E. Train, first chairman of the Council on Environmental Quality, that the act "demands no less than a revolution in the way we approach problems and make decisions."[2] And Federal Judge Henry J. Friendly remarked that NEPA "is so broad, yet so opaque that it will take even longer than usual to comprehend its impact."[3] Contrasting with these judgments is a minority

opinion that "NEPA is easy to grasp. Doing so however restricts one to talking about documents."[4]

Neither the text of NEPA nor the judgment of the majority of
persons who have worked with the act or given it serious study
supports the opinion that NEPA is easy to grasp or that its
product is no more than paperwork. This viewpoint totally
misconstrues NEPA and misinterprets the function of the environmental impact statement. The NEPA "document" or environmental impact statement is significant only as evidence
that agencies have observed the congressional intent regarding a national policy for the environment. To make the statement the end product of the act is plainly contrary not only to
the stated purposes of the act, but also to its legislative history.
The EIS can neither be understood nor properly evaluated if
treated as an end in itself; it was intended and should be
regarded as no more than a means to an end.

The NEPA Strategy

The end purpose of NEPA was to reorient national environmental policy. Explicit reorientation toward the six goals
enumerated in Section 101 of the act was regarded as necessary, because the traditional policies and practices of government had become major factors obstructing their attainment.
The damaging impact of public policies on the environment
was rarely intentional (with the possible exception of deliberate
destruction of "unwanted" species of animals and plants). More
often, damaging effects were inadvertent consequences of
efforts to adapt the environment to human purposes.

The invention of the EIS to ensure that the goals of NEPA
would be taken seriously was necessitated by ad hoc uncoordinated lawmaking by the Congress and politically selective use
of science by the agencies. Over the decades the Congress had
expanded the roles of government in activities having major
environmental consequences. But characteristically these
roles and the authorizations accorded the agencies were single-
purpose or unilinear, without regard to the possibility of multi-

ple and unforeseen consequences. For example, authorization of the St. Lawrence Seaway did not take into account possible incursions of oceanic fish such as lamprey eels into the Great Lakes, nor did irrigation projects in the Rio Grande valley consider the possible destructive spread of the salt cedar, among other ecological changes.

There were logical explanations for the failure of public authorizations to provide for foreseeable possibilities and to take appropriate action to prevent or mitigate undesired side effects. The first was inherent in professional specialized expertise. Scientists and engineers whose skills were elicited in program and project planning had been trained along disciplinary lines with attention focused on phenomena directly pertinent to their disciplines. Scientific expertise was largely analytic and reductionist—skilled in the identification of "lowest common denominators." Concern with the integration and synthesis of scientific findings, especially with findings drawn from different disciplines, was largely relegated to academic studies and seldom affected policy decisions. Large projects required multidisciplinary inputs. But it was only fortuitous if contributions from the respective disciplines cumulated to a mutually consistent whole and did not omit significant areas of relevance. The ultimate decisionmakers, legislative or administrative, were seldom offered information needed to make policy determinations that would strike balances among all major values and considerations. And environmental values were largely precluded from consideration, in the normal process of program planning, by the perceived missions of the agencies and interpretations of their powers.

The second explanation for lack of agency attention to the environmental impacts of their actions may be found in the way their statutory mandates were written and interpreted. But here one encounters a paradox. Following the principle that the United States is a government of laws, not of men, public agencies have no power to act except as authorized by law. Thus, prior to NEPA, federal agencies often rejected pleas for environment protection or mitigation measures in their plans and programs on grounds of insufficient authority. Yet

over the years the Congress had added to the specific powers
conferred upon the agencies with little regard to their possible
interrelationship. A consequence of this practice was to provide
a legal foundation for agency action far in excess of any specific
legislative authorization.

Agencies found that through combining specific incremental authorizations, sometimes with multiple agency collaboration, the powers of government could be enormously expanded
for purposes not readily deducible from any specified powers
separately considered. Agencies thus could plead "no power"
where environmental protection or enhancement was concerned but could greatly expand their activities through projects for which no specific public authorization had ever been
obtained. For example, Southwest Power, a huge energy complex, was put together by combining the authorities of several
different public and private agencies under leadership of the
Bureau of Reclamation.[5]

By 1960 the great federal agencies, particularly those
charged with responsibilities pertaining to land use, natural
resources, and transportation, had become decisive in determining the nation's environmental future. The Bureau of Reclamation, the Corps of Engineers, the Department of
Agriculture, and the Federal Highway Administration, directly and by contract, had become major shapers of the national landscape. On-site transformation of the environment
was often the work of land developers, public utilities, and
corporate enterprises in agriculture, chemistry, forestry, mining, and manufacturing. But before any of these agents of
change could act upon the environment, some permitting or
facilitating act of government was almost invariably required.
The issuance of permits, licenses, approvals, the making of
loans, grants, or contracts, and the review of compliance with
various health and safety standards made many federal agencies, in effect, partners in private corporate enterprises.

These administrative acts also made the federal agencies
accessory to activities following from them that, among other
consequences, often degraded the quality of the environment.
For example, before a power line could cross a wilderness area,
before a coastal estuary could be dredged and backfilled to

create a marina, before a power plant could be sited and constructed, or a historic house bulldozed for a highway, federal action was required. And so if a national policy to protect the quality of the environment were to be effective, it needed somehow to include both private and public initiatives, which were increasingly being tied together by various legal requirements having little or nothing to do with environmental protection. The most simple and direct way to make a comprehensive policy for environmental protection effective was to make the federal agencies fully accountable for their actions that significantly affected the quality of the human environment (thereby also extending some measure of policy control over the private sector).

Establishment and enforcement of such accountability was essential to the effective implementation of NEPA. But how could this be accomplished when each agency acted under its own statutory mandate? The development of what may be called "the NEPA strategy" unfolded in a dialogue between Senator Henry M. Jackson, chairman of the Senate Committee on Interior and Insular Affairs, and me, as chief witness for the committee, on 16 April 1969 at the hearing on S.1075, the bill that was to become the National Environmental Policy Act.[6]

In the course of discussion, Senator Jackson said: "I am wondering if we might not broaden the policy provision in the bill so as to lay down a general requirement that would be applicable to all agencies that have responsibilities that affect the environment rather than going through agency by agency....If we try to go through all of the agencies that are now exercising certain responsibilities pursuant to law in which there is no environmental policy or standard laid out, we could be engaged in a recodification of the Federal statutes for a long, long time....I am trying to avoid a recodification of all of the statutes."[7] In response, I agreed that this problem "required specific action on the part of the Congress, because what we are talking about...is modifying or amending existing mandates to the agencies."[8]

To resolve the problem, a strategy was required that would overcome agency disclaimers of power to take account of environmental impacts and would also force agencies to consider

the possible impacts of their actions before the event and with
due regard to alternative means to accomplish their authorized
purposes. To accomplish these purposes three provisions were
written into the act.

First, with respect to want of authority, Section 103 required
that all federal agencies "shall review their present statutory
authority, administrative regulations, and current policies and
procedures for the purpose of determining whether there are
any deficiencies or inconsistencies therein which prohibit full
compliance with the purposes and provisions of this Act and
shall propose to the President not later than July 1, 1971, such
measures as may be necessary to bring their authority and
policies into conformity with the intent, purposes and procedures set forth in this Act." Confronted with this ultimatum,
no agency declared itself unable to comply with NEPA—but by
tacitly admitting power to comply, the agencies estopped themselves from future claims of legal inability to conform to NEPA.

Second, to demolish the want-of-power argument, Section
105 of NEPA declared that "the policies and goals set forth in
this Act are supplementary to those set forth in existing authorizations of Federal agencies." Thus, as I suggested to Senator
Jackson, the mandates of all federal agencies were amended by
NEPA, its provisions now becoming a part of the statutory law
governing every agency.

Third was a procedural reform—the EIS requirement. The
need here was for a provision, applicable to all federal agencies,
that would cause them to observe the policy goals of NEPA by
opening their actions to court review if they failed to do so. The
EIS was simultaneously a disclosure document and a decision-
focused document, but it was more. In effect, it forced a restructuring of the uses of information—notably scientific information—in the processes of agency planning and decisionmaking.
Without this strategy there was nothing to compel the agencies
to give more than token recognition to the purposes and provisions of NEPA. At the 16 April hearing I argued for including
in NEPA "an action-forcing operational aspect."

To declare a policy, I said, required "a statement which is so
written that it is capable of implementation; that it is not

merely a statement of things hoped for; not merely a statement of desirable goals or objectives; but that it is a statement which will compel or reinforce or assist all of these things." I argued "that a statement of policy by the Congress should at least consider measures to require the Federal agencies, in submitting proposals, to contain within the proposals an evaluation of the effect of these proposals upon the state of the environment, that in the licensing procedures of the various agencies such as the Atomic Energy Commission, or the Federal Power Commission or the Federal Aviation Agency there should also be...certain requirements with respect to environmental protection."[9] This suggestion was subsequently embodied in Section 102(2)(c) of NEPA requiring "in every recommendation or report on proposals for legislation and other major Federal actions significantly affecting the quality of the human environment, a detailed statement" regarding the impact of the proposed action on the environment.

It should now be apparent why this brief statute has been described as sophisticated, revolutionary, and opaque. It should also be apparent why the EIS was not a mere afterthought or a ritual exercise in documentation. Properly understood, NEPA is exceptionally coherent. It declares a policy which it illustrates by example, specifies procedural means toward achievement of this policy, and provides institutional arrangements and jurisdictional safeguards to ensure that these procedures and the objectives they serve will not be lost in the complex interactions between politics and bureaucracy.

The NEPA strategy belongs to a type of legislation that has been called ends-oriented agency forcing. In their study of the Clean Air Act of 1970, Bruce A. Ackerman and William T. Hassler compare two contrasting legislative approaches to ensure agency response to policy intent:

> Agency inaction can be cured in two different ways. The first, and more primitive, may be called "means-oriented" agency-forcing. Here the agency is told precisely which regulatory means should be used to reach the congressional objective.... Under the second form of agency-forcing, Congress requires the

agency to define its *ends* aggressively and challenges the agency
to select a course that promises to reach its goals effectively....
Unlike its competitor, "ends-oriented" agency-forcing does not
require Congress to indulge in instrumental judgments beyond
its capacity. Instead, it generates a process by which the ultimate aims of environmental policy can be clarified over time.[10]

The variant of ends-oriented agency forcing introduced by
NEPA was the procedural device of the impact statement. The
EIS did not prescribe technical means or standards to achieve
NEPA's goals, but it required a procedure to force agency
administrators to show that they had kept those goals in mind
in their planning and decisionmaking. Thus, unlike some of
the more criticized provisions of the antipollution statutes,
NEPA provided a flexible strategy that permitted experimentation and learning. The strict legal standard of compliance
required by NEPA pertained only to the procedure designed to
keep the ends specified by the act in the forefront of agency
policy and action.

Science and NEPA

Science, however defined, as customarily employed by governments has tended to be specialized, reductionist, and linear.
Attack upon environmental problems requires interdisciplinary synthesizing approaches for which multidisciplinary planning alone is inadequate in concept and method. Thus a critical
element in the strategy of NEPA has been Section 102 of the
act, which states in part that "the Congress authorizes and
directs that, to the fullest extent possible...all agencies of the
Federal Government shall...utilize a systematic, interdisciplinary approach which will insure the integrated use of
the natural and social sciences and environmental design arts
in planning and decisionmaking which may have an impact on
man's environment [and]...initiate and utilize ecological information in the planning and development of resource-oriented
projects."

Neither of these requirements was self-executing, and neither corresponded to the normal, routine analyses undertaken by the agencies. Effective attack upon environmental problems and assessments of the environmental impacts of federal actions required the interdisciplinary approach and the integrated use of science set forth in NEPA. The EIS was, in part, designed to obtain agency compliance with these requirements. It is not (or more properly was not) difficult to point out instances when agency performance under NEPA has fallen short of the drafters' intentions. Nevertheless, evidence reported in subsequent chapters of this book—and the evidence is increasing—indicates that agency handling of the EIS or NEPA process has improved with experience and that its purpose is now generally understood as a tool of policy analysis and an integral phase of planning. It has become the most important single means for ensuring the involvement of the appropriate kind of science in the NEPA process.

The environmental impact statement is not a scientific document, nor does the statute specify the use of science in its preparation. But use of science is implicit in the impact statement because the five points upon which the act requires the agencies to report findings could not be adequately addressed without recourse to science. This practical necessity became an explicit requirement under *Regulations for Implementing the Procedural Provisions of NEPA* issued in 1978 by the Council on Environmental Quality.[11]

The integrated use of science as required in Section 102(2)(a) of NEPA was explicitly joined to the preparation of impact statements by the regulations (e.g., Section 1502.6) and was reinforced by other provisions regarding the uses of science, especially Section 1502.24 on methodology and scientific accuracy. Section 1500.3 declares that "the regulations apply to the whole of Section 102(2) [of the statute]. The provisions of the Act and these regulations must be read together as a whole in order to comply with the spirit and letter of the law." Thus the statute and its implementing regulations built into the agencies' procedures uses of science intended to direct plan-

ning and decisionmaking toward the broad purposes declared
in the initial sections of the act.

NEPA's use of procedures to restructure and redirect science
as a major input into policy and decisionmaking has implications that extend beyond the act. The strategy could be applied
to other areas of public policy and administration in which
information is critical. In our society, knowledge described as
"scientific" is playing an increasingly important role in public
affairs. How this knowledge is used is therefore of utmost
importance. Knowledge misapplied may be harmful; short of
that it is misleading. We cannot (and never could) safely assume that the "right" knowledge automatically finds its way
into policy. The uses of knowledge must be managed not merely
through systems of information gathering, storage, analysis,
and retrieval. The scope, content, and application of the information must also be managed.

Risk to intellectual freedom and to the unbiased use of
information is always inherent in the "management" of knowledge. Yet in one way or another knowledge of social significance
is always managed by someone, and this may be most safely
and fairly done when the management is explicit and publicly
accountable. To a significant degree, therefore, this book may
be read as a study in official accountability, focused upon an
aspect of public administration in which the uses of science in
the planning and decision processes have been redirected toward goals previously unspecified in law and policy.

Even a cursory review of published discourse and debate on
science policy and NEPA reveals a pattern of semantic confusion—of issues imperfectly joined because their protagonists
had no mutually agreed-upon terms of reference. Clarity in
discussing the uses of science in the reform of administrative
procedures requires clarification of the meanings attributed to
science, administrative procedures, and reform. These terms
may be understood in widely varying ways. Other meanings
may be legitimate, but specifying how these terms are used
here should assist the reader in understanding the relationships among them described in the following chapters.

Four Faces of Science

The universe of potential knowledge is undefined and, we may assume, unknown. What we do know has been categorized into divisions that we call disciplines. Although in theory there is a universal body of knowledge that may be called science, in fact there are many sciences, and the extent to which individual sciences have matured and advanced varies greatly, as does the degree of complexity among them. There is no need here to attempt a discrimination between basic and applied science or between so-called hard and soft sciences. As used in this book, science, unmodified, relates only to the ways in which the term is used in ordinary public discourse without benefit of philosophical refinement.

To attempt a concise and generally accepted definition of science would be impractical. As a generalization it is sufficient to say that "science," as used here, is the primary object of concern to the National Academy of Sciences, the National Science Foundation, and the American Association for the Advancement of Science. Obviously, not everyone associated with these institutions understands "science" in the same way, but only in exceptional cases do these differences cause major difficulties.

In ordinary discourse, science is a multifaceted term that presents at least four different aspects. With equal propriety it is used to refer to (1) method, (2) occupation, (3) knowledge, and (4) application. As commonly used, it tends to be an amalgam of all four, but at particular places in the following discussion it may be used primarily with respect to one or another of these meanings. The particular meaning should be apparent from the context. The term "science" in the vernacular represents a cultural, not a scientific, concept. Distinctions between basic and applied science and between the latter and engineering are sometimes significant, but require no special attention in relation to the concerns of this book.

Scientific propositions are often described as hypotheses that are subject to disproof. Popular and political usage is less precise, however, with "science" being more often understood simply as knowledge derived empirically from recorded experience or from experiment as contrasted with knowledge attributed solely to inspiration or revelation. Many sciences are, of course, classified in different ways—physical, biological, social, hard, soft—and there are so-called border or quasi-sciences.

Science, meaning method, has generated a large literature that cannot be summarized here. For our purposes it suffices to define scientific methods as those that increase knowledge by systematic use of theory, observation, measurement, and logic—methods that subject potential knowledge to testing. Persons who devise and apply "scientific methods" may be called scientists, but this term (or its counterpart in various languages) may be more specifically applied in particular societies. It may be applied, as in the United States, primarily to professional practitioners in particular disciplines, such as physics, using methods of inquiry (notably quantitative) that are regarded as "scientific." Thus "scientists" are people whose investigations employ scientific methods, and the methods used by persons recognized as scientists are accepted by many people as "scientific." The meaning of "science" is less a matter of logic and more a reflection of cultural attitudes. Analogous expressions in French and Russian, for example, are more broadly defined.

Science in the vernacular is an abstract concept. To reduce science to concrete examples we must turn to the scientific disciplines, ranging from agronomy to zoology. The concept of a "discipline" is important to an understanding of two major themes in this book. The first is the explicit commitment in NEPA to "a systematic, interdisciplinary approach" and an "integrated use of the natural and social sciences." The second is that this interdisciplinary approach, reinforced by NEPA, but strengthened also by other forces, is leading to a new level of integration of knowledge called "environmental science."

The growth of knowledge has been characterized by two contrasting yet complementary trends—the subdivision of knowledge into ever more specialized, discrete disciplines and the integration of knowledge into more inclusive and complex levels of generality. This dual development has been essential to the advancement of knowledge, but specialization and the reduction of knowledge to descriptions of ever more elementary or basic phenomena have proceeded more rapidly than has integration. Explanation of why integration appears to be more difficult than reduction, and why it has lagged behind, is beyond the scope of this discussion. Integration cannot occur until there is something to integrate. The accumulation of factual knowledge is a necessary precursor of its synthesis. But when synthesis does occur, new knowledge may also be created—the whole being more than the parts.

It is for this reason that the architects of NEPA asked for an interdisciplinary approach. The objective was not to mobilize relevant sciences and to focus each in its own way on environmental problems. What was sought through NEPA was a joining of sciences in relationships that would fill the informational or conceptual interspaces between the various sciences. This purpose was born out of a growing conviction among many scientists and administrators that efforts to understand the complex interrelationships of natural systems would succeed only when matched by a coherent systematization of knowledge that corresponded to the substance and behavior of the phenomenon under investigation.

NEPA was needed because modern society, especially in the United States, increasingly undertook to intrude upon and to attempt to manage complex systems, man-made and natural, with fractional and uncoordinated pieces of knowledge drawn from the disciplines. Science was coherent primarily at the disciplinary level, but the environmental problems that society was creating were at levels of generality exceeding the reach of any discipline. NEPA accordingly represents an effort to transcend disciplinary limitations and to influence the development of science toward more inclusive levels of interrelationship and coherence.

To the extent that an integrated approach is required on the job and, through practical necessity, scientists in government learn what it means to be interdisciplinary and to demonstrate

how the product of interdisciplinary effort differs from uni-
disciplinary or multidisciplinary approaches, the structure
and methods of science may be affected. There may be limits to
the capacity of humans for integrative thought, but there is no
evidence that they have been reached. Thus it does not appear
to be a mere figure of speech to say that environmental science
is a new level of integrative knowledge toward which NEPA has
made a significant contribution.

This brief excursion into the semantics of science may be
summarized by saying that science is (1) *method* (in fact, a
body of methodology) for creating and testing knowledge. It is
developed and used as (2) an *occupation* by "scientists" who
seek to establish a body of (3) *knowledge* (i.e., tested fact and
theory), which is often referred to as "science." Finally, as
previously noted, a distinction is sometimes drawn between so-
called "pure" or basic science and its (4) *application* to human
needs and purposes. And so it is knowledge, derived by professional scientists through methods believed to be scientific and
applied to public affairs, with which we are primarily concerned. But the application of science required by NEPA is not
the discrete, specialized knowledge organized by the disciplines. It is interdisciplinary, not multidisciplinary, knowledge
and represents an effort to achieve new levels of informational
and conceptual integration. The distinction is between disciplinary knowledge integrated into a coherent matrix but with
missing interstitial data identified (and perhaps remedied), as
contrasted with separate and uncoordinated inputs from the
disciplines to the analysis of a policy problem with greater risk
of missing data being undisclosed.

Administrative Procedures

In these chapters "administrative procedures" include all
actions by public authorities that translate basic policy as
expressed through statute or other legislative means into action. Thus neither the term "administrative" nor "procedure" is
to be understood in the more specialized meanings sometimes

given them in writings on administrative law. The usage here is relatively loose and general.

During recent decades, administration by the judiciary, especially the federal judiciary, has increased prodigiously. The federal courts have shown more restraint in the area of environmental policy than in some other policy areas; that is, they have generally been less willing than, say, in civil rights, to substitute their judgments for those of the agencies.[12] But in the absence of clear and consistent presidential leadership, the burden of interpreting the National Environmental Policy Act has fallen largely to them. Thus the role of the courts in the NEPA process mandated by Section 102 must be considered as belonging to the total process of administering the act although that role will be considered here primarily as it bears upon major questions of procedural reform in relation to policy.

Thus "administration" as used here is comprehensively defined—it is not less than the implementation of policy. Policies are, of course, generated and revised during the process of implementation. I do not regard the term "administration" as amenable to unequivocal, precise definition. Particular shades of meaning which the term may take on at particular points in the text should be evident from the context in which the term is used.

Semantics of Reform

In the conventional language of politics, everyone "understands" the word reform, and that is why the term requires examination. What everyone understands is usually imperfectly defined at a very high level of generalization. Probably to most people "reform" is synonymous with "throw the rascals out" or "clean up corruption." In fact, these actions are only means to an end that is the true objective of reform. More precisely defined, reform means to reshape or restructure. Reformation may therefore be understood as a means to an end: action taken to redirect policies or priorities. Beyond this relatively neutral meaning—the nature of the change unspecified—reform carries a normative connotation and the suggestion that the sought-for change is morally desirable.

The environmental movement has been directed toward reform and hence has had a moral or ethical content, its underlying assumption being that it is inherently wrong to impair, especially unnecessarily, the quality of the environment. This moral or ethical bias toward quality is evident in the literature of environmental protection issues, and it has made compromise difficult in many environmental controversies. From the perspective of environmental protectionists, and equally perhaps from the different perspectives of their opponents, the choices are clearly between right and wrong. This atmosphere of moral conviction has characteristically surrounded political controversies involving the environment and has often been relied upon to obtain compliance with declared principles. But although principles were declared in the National Environmental Policy Act (Section 101), their persuasiveness was not relied upon by the drafters to accomplish the task of administrative reform as a means toward redirection of national policy.

NEPA Pro and Con

The foregoing discussion of concepts and terminology does not address one aspect of NEPA that could be confusing to readers. This is the anti-NEPA literature, some of which is incorporated in attacks upon the environmental protection movement generally. Although not numerous, the anti-NEPA writings are vigorous and unequivocal. Readers otherwise uninformed about NEPA might well infer that the act was "a disaster in the environmental movement"[13] or that the EIS was intended to pacify "the demands of ecologically concerned citizens" because "many politicians have been quick to grasp that the quickest way to silence critical 'ecofreaks' is to allocate small proportions of funds for any engineering project for ecological studies."[14]

Much of the criticism may be described as editorializing unsupported by evidence of actual performance under the act. Claims of NEPA's burdensome ineffectuality have characteristically been little more than repetitions of tendentious studies exploiting a "worst case" situation. Almost never have these adversarial critics shown evidence of having evaluated the findings of oversight committees of the Congress or reports by the General Accounting Office, the Commission on Federal Paperwork, and the Council on Environmental Quality. I know of no instance in which a hostile critic has personally investigated a significant number of government offices in which environmental analysis was actually being done. When queried about these omissions, adversaries have often responded that data derived from government personnel are obviously untrustworthy—biased in favor of NEPA. But adversaries have also largely ignored the findings of authors of scholarly and objectively critical studies of NEPA and commentaries in leading casebooks on environmental law. References to these works may be found in the Bibliographical Note.

Are the merits and demerits of NEPA mere matters of opinion? There are sharply opposing assessments of the significance and effectiveness of NEPA, but they appear to be heavily one-sided. The majority opinion regards NEPA as highly significant and generally effective, albeit, as with all human effort, subject to varying degrees of misinterpretation or misuse. The adversary minority regards NEPA as worse than ineffective, indeed, a counterproductive imposition on government and the economy. Who, then, is entitled to belief?

The position taken in this book is positive but not uncritical. NEPA is presented as an innovative and creative effort to redirect national policy as it affects the quality of the environment. The environmental impact statement was devised to overcome anticipated resistance to the redefinition of agency responsibility required by the act. The EIS is the key element in a process designed to obtain compliance with congressional intent as expressed throughout the act. But the EIS is only part of NEPA, although the part that activates the whole.

It should have been evident to objective assessors of NEPA that its implementation would require a learning process and experience over time. The understanding, the experience, the organizational arrangements, and the personnel to achieve NEPA goals and standards were not in place when administration of the act commenced. Misconstruction and misuse of the EIS was to be expected. For a valid test, NEPA's effectiveness would have to be appraised over some period of time. The early evaluations often focused on errors made in the course of learning. The *Regulations* issued by the CEQ in late 1978 and effective in July 1979 reflected the learning that had occurred during the better part of a decade. They addressed nearly every criticism previously brought against NEPA. Most of these were relevant only to performance during the early and middle 1970s when agencies were learning how to adapt to the requirements of the act and especially how to make the EIS the effective tool of planning and decisionmaking that its authors intended.

The courts' early determination that NEPA should apply retroactively to unfinished federal projects meant that many of the first EISs applied to projects predating NEPA goals, provisions, or criteria. At the outset of NEPA implementation, the EIS process was often embarrassed by having to cope with the environmental demerits of projects that were nearing completion. These projects often reflected a lack of environmental sensitivity characteristic of the years preceding the environmental movement of the 1960s. It was often difficult to apply the systematic interdisciplinary analysis that NEPA required to fait accompli projects, and there was seldom an incentive to do so beyond that required by the letter of the law. The NEPA process was fully applicable only to new projects.

The ultimate importance of NEPA lies in its declared goals. The policy is paramount; the means, however innovative or interesting, are incidental. They exist because, as Ackerman and Hassler observe, "Environmentalists were right in trying to assure that this outpouring of public sentiment [in the late 1960s] would not be sabotaged by administrative passivity. The idea of agency-forcing was a legal innovative response to this need."[15] The goals of NEPA were never self-executing.

How far do these goals extend? The statement of purpose includes "efforts which will prevent or eliminate damage to the environment and the biosphere," and Section 102(2) (f) requires the federal agencies to "recognize the worldwide and long-range character of environmental problems and, where consistent with the foreign policy of the United States, lend appropriate support to initiatives, resolutions, and programs designed to maximize international cooperation in anticipating and preventing decline in the quality of mankind's world environment."

Controversy has arisen over these provisions and because NEPA nowhere exempts the actions of the federal agencies falling outside of United States territorial jurisdiction from the requirements of the act. The contention has been over the applicability of NEPA to actions occurring in other countries and upon the high seas.[16] The language of NEPA would seem to remove all doubt unless the phrase "consistent with the foreign policy" is interpreted to provide an a priori exemption to extraterritorial activities of agencies such as the Departments of State, Defense, and Agriculture and the Export-Import Bank. It seems clear that some agency actions that have major and damaging environmental impacts do not fall under NEPA—military operations considered essential to national defense, for example. Nevertheless, the question has arisen: To what extent do United States agencies have the right and responsibility to assess, report, and recommend concerning the impacts of their actions upon foreign countries or upon the biosphere generally?

This question was answered largely by implication in President Jimmy Carter's Executive Order 12114, signed 4 January 1979, entitled "Environmental Effects Abroad of American Federal Actions." In principle, the United States has bound itself by certain statutory laws in addition to NEPA and by several treaties to assume responsibilities declared also by NEPA and consistent with both customary and positive international law. As examples, the Convention for the Preservation and Protection of Fur Seals of 1911, the Convention on Nature Protection and Wildlife Preservation in the Western Hemisphere of 1942, the Convention on International Trade in Endangered Species of Wild Flora and Fauna of 1976, the Marine Mammals Protection Act of 1972, and the Marine Protection, Research, and Sanctuaries Act of 1972 may be cited. Disagreement, however, still surrounds the question of the extent to which American domestic environmental policies should bind American government and business abroad.

The basic responsibility is to observe a long-standing principle of international law to which the United States has repeatedly acceded and specifically endorsed in the 1972 Resolutions of the United Nations Conference on the Human Environment that a state ought not use its territory in a manner that would be damaging to the health, welfare, and safety of other nations. The United States had previously insisted on the observance of this principle in the Trail Smelter controversy with Canada, and the principle is also embodied in the Boundary Waters Treaty of 1909 with Canada.

The effect of NEPA on other nations is little different from the policy adopted by the World Bank of requiring some analysis of environmental impacts in the consideration of loans for projects that might result in significant, avoidable environmental damage. The application of NEPA to international activities of United States federal agencies at most restricts what they may do on the territory of other nations directly or indirectly. NEPA in no way imposes American standards, values, or objectives upon the governments of other nations. They are absolutely free to proceed with whatever projects they think best. There is no apparent reason why the United States should act abroad, in violation of principles and procedures established for its own conduct, to assist projects that might either have a deleterious effect upon the neighbors of countries in which the project was undertaken or upon substantial numbers of people in the host country either now or in the future. It has been a matter of common knowledge that governments everywhere, including Third World governments, have often been manipulated by unrepresentative, self-seeking internal interests to obtain international financial assistance for projects that are ecologically and often even economically undesirable. The United States government has been the object of Third World criticism, sometimes vociferous, as having promoted and assisted unsound projects to enlarge the Swiss bank accounts of Third World politicians and entrepreneurs. The United States, as well as other industrialized countries, has also been publicly faulted for using Third World territories to export its polluting industries and to dump its unwanted toxic substances or unsafe products.

Executive Order 12114 should therefore be seen as a clear exercise of responsibility on the part of the United States government that is consistent with the best principles of international conduct and is in no way prejudicial to the legitimate interests of other nations. The effectiveness of the order is debatable, but it is difficult to argue against its intent if one accepts the declared purpose of NEPA. It may be better to be criticized for cultural imperialism by Third World politicians than to be the object of legitimate popular outrage. The reputation of the United States would suffer more for involvement in the failure of a massive dam in India or the poisoning of the people in the countryside of Sierra Leone because its administrators took an indulgent view of aid requests and were so respectful of the sovereignty of the host country and its right to make its own mistakes that they became party to international tragedy.

Whatever the fate of Executive Order 12114 may be under the Reagan administration, the ethical principle underlying the order cannot be abrogated. Nor can the specific mandates of NEPA be ignored without dereliction of constitutional duty. The acceptance in the declarations and statutes of many other countries of the same principles that NEPA enunciates makes observance of the guidance afforded by Executive Order 12114 an evidence of international "good citizenship." Again it is the policy that is important: respect for the environment and the biosphere evidenced by ascertaining, so far as feasible, the effect of public action on the world of which man is a part and by searching for the least damaging alternatives to the satisfaction of human needs.

Contrary to occasional assertions of critics, the environmental movement did not appear out of nowhere and NEPA was not mainly the product of an alleged environmental hysteria that swept America in the late 1960s and early 1970s. Both NEPA and the environmental movement, of which it was an expression, had historical antecedents extending backward over many decades. Because this history, especially that part of it relating to the conservation movement, has been recounted elsewhere there is no need to repeat it here.[17] But because NEPA and the environmental movement resulted from the convergence of several historical trends, perspective on the act requires some reference to its conceptual roots. Important among these is the relationship between government and science. The development of this relationship and its ultimate effect upon the demand for an environmental policy is the subject of the next chapter.

2
Using Science in Planning and Decisionmaking

Passage of the National Environmental Policy Act of 1969 marked a change in the customary relationship between government and science. For more than three hundred years in Western society—more recently in America—government had been the patron and employer of science and its handmaiden, technology. But by mid-twentieth century some unforeseen consequences of the success of this relationship raised doubts about the unqualified reliability of science as servant of public welfare. As it became evident that the benefits of science were accompanied by risks, unquestioned belief in these benefits began to be qualified by doubts.

The atom bomb was the most obvious symbol of the risks. But the risks were most directly apparent in the environmental consequences of the day-to-day uses of science and technology in a rapidly expanding economy. Many of these consequences revealed, in the words of President Lyndon B. Johnson, "the dark side of technology." Many were directly linked to government efforts to promote economic growth. The massive interstate highway system, for example, had the unforeseen effect of destroying urban neighborhoods and rural landscapes. Government-subsidized water and power projects generated environmentally damaging chains of consequences over large areas of the country.

Thus the environmental movement of the 1960s and thereafter was more than a generalized effort to reform the behavior of man toward nature. Pursuant to this larger objective, it was also an effort to restate the priorities and responsibilities of government. Increasingly, the adverse effects of science and technology on the quality of life were seen as failures of success—failure of the government as partner in the science-technology relationship to take responsible account of the consequences of technoscientific developments to which it was a party that, though beneficial in intent, often led to unwanted and unforeseen consequences.

Other aspects of the environmental movement were directed toward the economy generally and entailed regulations in the private sector. But the National Environmental Policy Act was focused specifically upon the role of the federal government in shaping and protecting the environment. The task set for its authors was to redirect national policy toward the environment; the method was procedural reform.

The Government-Science Connection

Attempts to apply reliable knowledge to public purposes appear to be as old as government itself. Environmental forecasting is at least as old as priestly calculations of the rise and fall of the Nile. In almost every historical culture savants were brought together in the courts of rulers. Environmental events affecting agriculture and military affairs were invariably high on the agenda of official concern. But not until the mid-seventeenth century did governments begin to employ knowledge, tested sufficiently to be called "science," in a systematic and policy-oriented way. Notably in the court of Louis XIV, but also in the governments of other national states emerging in Europe, the selective use of scientific knowledge became a distinguishing attribute of centralizing government.[1] Mobilization of science in the service of the state became a hallmark of modernity.

Under the direction of the Great Elector in Brandenburg-Prussia, cameralism institutionalized state surveillance over the economy and natural resources. In France, Louis's master administrator Colbert saw science as a centralizing instrument of national power. Louis saw in science a role for royal patronage, magnifying and glorifying the state of which he was the personification. Colbert understood that science under official tutelage could strengthen the military and economic power of the state. Thus establishment of the French Academy of Sciences in 1662 made official a relationship between government and science that has ramified to transform the world and forms an important link in the chain of events leading to the environmental role of government in our own time. And so, in modernizing, centralizing European government, patronage of science began a developing relationship between science and society that inevitably was to become more broadly political. As the concerns of society and government became more numerous and complex and the scope and reliability of science increased, the government-science connection grew in importance.

In the beginning there was no clear division between public or official science and private or unofficial science—a distinction, often imperfect, that developed largely in the nineteenth century with the growth of private and corporate support for scientific inquiry. In England, for example, and with subsequent implications for science in America, King Charles II chartered the Royal Society but did not make it an official arm of the state. Government in Great Britain never undertook the centralizing, directing role in the economy that characterized the absolutist regimes on the European continent. Those governments followed the French example. In 1725 Czar Peter I of Russia established the Russian Academy of Sciences, which is ancestral to the present-day Academy of Sciences in the USSR.

The informal and ambiguous relationship between official and unofficial science in eighteenth-century Britain carried over into the British colonies in North America. Shapers of the American political ethos, such as Thomas Jefferson, tended to favor an encouraging but generally nonparticipatory role for government in the advancement of science. Alexander Hamilton, following the model of Colbert, would have had government play a more positive role in the use of science to develop manufacturing and the arts. More than half a century was to elapse, however, before the new American republic was to play a significant role as policymaker in relation to science.

In the relationship of government to science, explicit patronage should be distinguished from mere encouragement. The distinction emerged in differences between Hamilton and Jefferson over the most effective way for government to encourage inventions. Hamilton leaned toward direct government bounties and awards; Jefferson favored private reward through the market protected by patent rights. Until the Civil War, sectional conflict and constitutional uncertainties restrained federal patronage of science. The Smithsonian Institution was established in 1846 through a private British bequest that was accepted only after years of political opposition in the Senate of the United States. Explicit involvement of the United States government in setting priorities in science began in 1862 with congressional establishment through the first Morrill Act of a national system of land grants on behalf of public colleges for agriculture and mechanical arts. With passage of this act, the Congress had moved from mere encouragement to patronage and thereafter increasingly became both a client of scientific investigators and an inadvertent setter of priorities and directions in scientific work.

Whatever their position regarding relationships with science and scientists, modern governments found science useful, and most of them therefore engaged to some extent in the promotion of science. In Britain, for example, where government remained an indirect and somewhat aloof benefactor, the interests of commerce and navigation were sufficiently important to justify royal support for even so extramundane a science as astronomy. Practical considerations of political economy determined that there would be an "astronomer royal" in Britain and that time-telling throughout the world would be calculated in relation to scientific instruments and observations based at Greenwich (e.g., Greenwich Mean Time, G.M.T.). In France, applied science lay beyond the self-imposed limits of university concern, and Napoleon therefore moved to meet the needs of an energetic state through the science-based school of engineering known as the Ecole Polytechnique.[2] In Austria, France, and the Netherlands, statistics—the systematic collection and analysis of data that concerned the state—was accorded official status as a tool of national policymaking.[3] Thus science, as method, became a conventional instrument of government policy. But science, as knowledge not visibly related to the practical concerns of the day, received little official notice. Science, as occupation, played little role in the testing and implementation of policy decisions. With relatively few exceptions, it was not until well into the nineteenth century that science as a professional occupation emerged as distinguishable from science as a personal avocation.

Throughout all modern Western societies there has been a tendency to regard science as a "servant": to admire it because of its practical utility, because "it works." But popular attitudes have been changing as applications of science-based technology have led to consequences clouding the optimism with which scientific progress traditionally has been regarded. Throughout America and Western Europe people have increasingly realized that it is easier to command science to act than to control the consequences of an unqualified command. As in the parable of the sorcerer's apprentice, society has been learning that to invoke the aid of science with incomplete or inadequate instructions is to incur the risk of undesired consequences. Although the managers of modern science, in government and out, have never questioned Francis Bacon's dictum that "nature to be commanded must be obeyed," they have not always appreciated its implications. The "laws of nature" are not often obvious. But it often happens that nature cannot be obeyed until its laws are understood. To discover these laws is the task of scientific inquiry, which may vary greatly in scope and method in relation to that aspect of nature for which understanding is sought. Methods appropriate to elucidating relatively simple, invariant phenomena may be insufficient for revealing complex and variable phenomena, extended over time. Environmental relationships are largely of the latter type.

The past achievements of science have contributed primarily to understanding relatively less complex natural phenomena. Modern science has been mainly reductionist, aimed at learning more and more about the most basic and elementary aspects of nature. This emphasis on fundamentals has been a necessary precursor to the investigation of more complex systems and relationships. Yet the behavior of complex social and ecological systems cannot be deduced merely by aggregating their constituent parts. The "nature" within which human society lives and interacts is a grand synthesis; it cannot be safely commanded solely through recourse to reductionist concepts. To be understood sufficiently for guiding human action the interrelationships and interactions of man and nature must be understood as aspects of systems evolving over time. Yet no derogation of reductionist methods is implied. Without a solid foundation in the detailed substance of scientific knowledge there can be no valid synthesis.

Reductionist science addresses specific parts of the total environmental situation, but does not necessarily describe the interrelating of the parts and their integration into the findings upon which policy decisions could be based. In considering whether to dam a river the decisionmaker could request in-depth analyses from geologists on foundation properties of rock, from limnologists on aquatic biota, from soil scientists, hydrologists, and botanists on watershed effects, and from economists on monetary costs and benefits and still be unequipped to assess the impact of the dam on the environment. A scientific methodology would be needed that could assemble multi-disciplinary reductionist data, identify missing information, discover relationships previously unperceived, and develop a synthesis of these elements into findings or propositions upon which decisions could be made.[4]

Science in American Government

The history of science in America has been described in broader scope by Hunter Dupree and others.[5] Our concern here is only with those aspects of the government-science relationship that led to demands for more effective control over the uses of science in public planning and decisionmaking. During the pre—Civil War period there was little occasion for concern about the relationship; indeed there was little science to be concerned about. As government concern with science emerged, it was more to ensure man's mastery over nature than to understand the implications of human demands upon the natural world. There were, of course, exceptions to the utilitarian emphasis of public support for scientific inquiry. But the generality, not the exceptions, shaped government-science relationships.

Following the British tradition, early science in America was largely the avocation of learned gentlemen such as Benjamin Rush and David Rittenhouse. Science had been regarded as a branch of philosophy, and there had been little development and testing of theory. Such investigations as were undertaken would today be regarded as more in the nature of inventions or empirical experiments. With the possible exception of schools of medicine, there was no institutional structure for the advancement of science. The field of engineering arose in a practical way as an adjunct of military activities, the United States Army Corps of Engineers becoming the first agency for the development of engineering capability within the United States. Before the mid-nineteenth century men such as Alexander Bache and Joseph Henry had made science a public career.

During the first half century of national independence, the involvement of government with science grew and became more positive. An important reason was the challenge presented by the vast, largely unexplored areas of the trans-Mississippi West. Regarded broadly—as science should be regarded in relation to public policy—geographical exploration must be included as a science-related activity of government.

The Lewis and Clark expedition (1804–06) sponsored by President Thomas Jefferson was the beginning of official exploratory missions, a practice continued, for example, in Antarctica, on the moon, and still under way with the Voyager probes of the solar system. Although the initial linkage between geographical exploration and environmental policy (as later conceived) was not strong, the relevance of the growth of scientific understanding of the nature of the Earth and the growth of environmental awareness is apparent in retrospect. John Wesley Powell's explorations in the American Southwest (1867–74), for example, influenced subsequent policies relating to the environment of that region but were not always directed toward its protection. In the Antarctic Treaty of 1959 American policy more clearly supported an integration of scientific exploration and environmental protection. But behind all of these efforts, their potential contribution to material progress was a major consideration.

The Civil War was the first major watershed in the relationship between government and science in the United States. Following the withdrawal of southern constitutional conservatives from the Congress, two significant developments occurred. One was the establishment in 1863 of the National Academy of Sciences to provide the government with information and advice of practical utility. The other was the first Morrill Act of 1862, mentioned earlier, which laid the foundation for government science in agriculture and engineering.

In America, as in France, traditional higher education did not provide practical knowledge of importance to certain national needs; thus in allocating land grants to the states for the study of agriculture and the mechanical arts, the Congress took a large step toward a closer and more directive relationship with science. The Patent Office was playing an increasing role in government encouragement of private science. Public science, with environmental implications, expanded with establishment of the Geological Survey in 1879 and with the progressive expansion of public health services including passage of the Food and Drug Act in 1906. By the turn of the century, public and national concern with applied science and engineering included forestry, irrigation, and the development of mineral resources. In each of these policy areas science was invoked and scientists played leading roles.

Yet in comparison to what was to happen, the range of government concern for science, although growing, was comparatively narrow. For example, such responsibility as government undertook in the field of medical science was largely in relation to matters of military activity, immigration, and animal husbandry. Public health meant little more than public sanitation and quarantine, and although the quality of domestic water supply began to receive public attention, environmental concerns per se were narrowly limited.[6]

Although a federal department of science was proposed as early as 1885, the idea was not seriously considered. The nation's primary science agency—the U.S. Department of Agriculture (USDA)—did not obtain cabinet status until 1889. World War I brought about an expansion of the government-science relationship, but did not result in changes in that relationship as far-reaching as those following World War II.

Developments during World War II, and more especially the postwar launching of the Russian satellite Sputnik in 1957, marked a new major watershed in government-science relationships in America. After 1945 the federal government rapidly became a major patron of science and on a very large scale. New science and technological institutions were established: the Atomic Energy Commission (1946), the National Science Foundation (1950), and the National Aeronautics and Space Administration (1958). The National Institutes of Health, established in the 1940s, were greatly expanded. A special science adviser to the president was appointed in 1957, followed shortly by the reconstituting of the presidential Science Advisory Committee. A Federal Council for Science and Technology was formed in 1959 to improve coordination of the scientific and technical functions of the federal agencies.

This trend was not confined to the executive branch. "Science" increasingly appeared in the title or on the agendas of committees and subcommittees of the Congress. A number of these committees, notably the House Committee on Science and Astronautics, began to exercise an overview function respecting the direction and implications of science in America and the role and responsibility of the federal government in determining its future.

In 1970, establishment of the Council on Environmental Quality by statute, and of the Environmental Protection Agency (EPA) and the National Oceanic and Atmospheric

Administration (NOAA) by executive Reorganization Plans 3 and 4, not only exemplified an expanded involvement of science in government but also marked the institutionalizing of commitments by government to improve the quality of public decisionmaking through a more integrated, interdisciplinary use of scientific information and methodology. As the role of government in science expanded, organized concern appeared among scientists. In 1961 the National Academy of Sciences established a Committee on Science and Public Policy, and volunteer associations of scientists coalesced around such issues involving science policy as atomic weaponry and environmental hazards.

This growth in reliance upon science and in critical concern for its application was not without exceptions. The president who issued the reorganization orders establishing EPA and NOAA abolished the office of science adviser to the president. But the later action revealed an idiosyncrasy of Richard Nixon in relation to scientists that was no more than a minor reversal of the general trend. During the succeeding presidency, Congress restored the office by statutory law. Moreover, Reorganization Plans 3 and 4 of 1970 were not mere reshuffles for presidential convenience of existing science-related agencies. Each plan reflected, at least in part, studies by the Advisory Council on Executive Reorganization and the U.S. Commission on Marine Science, Engineering, and Resources of more effective ways to integrate the administration of functions that were heavily involved with applied science.

Major break-points can be identified, but for the greater part of its history the evolution of the relationship between government, science, and technology in America has been gradual and incremental. Only in retrospect is it clear that the Civil War and World War II were watersheds in the relationship; it would not have appeared obvious to most observers at those times. Nor is it apparent to many people today that 1970 and NEPA may have marked another watershed in the relationship. Some have perceived the redirecting of science for environmental analysis as a transitory anomaly, a temporary aberration that will ultimately pass away. But after more than a dozen years it is clear that the change, although incomplete and sometimes contradictory, is enduring.

Policymakers in government or business may yet choose to disregard scientific evidence in planning and decisionmaking, but they can no longer use science to manage the environment with no consideration of the consequences. The antienvironmentalist allegation that NEPA and the environmental movement generally reflect the inordinate influence of no more than a small, affluent, self-serving minority is not supported by the most solid evidence we have concerning public attitudes and values and their changes during the past decade. Results of a 1980 survey sponsored by several federal agencies indicated that public support for the environmental movement had remained strong throughout the decade and was broadly based.[7] Nuclear energy, however, is an issue over which environmentalist opinion has been polarized. Concern over nuclear fallout was one of the several issues around which the environmental movement initially formed. But on the energy issue environmentalists divided, antinuclear protest becoming the signal behavior of the radical end of the environmentalist spectrum. For many people, however, controlling science and technology was the primary issue; nuclear technology was only one of many environmental problems and not necessarily the most urgent among them.

Reaction against the exponential expansion of government-supported science began even while that expansion was occurring, within less than two decades following World War II. Concern over the effects of nuclear radiation was an initial catalytic factor but others were to follow. There had always been dissenters during the three hundred years of largely uncritical optimism regarding the beneficence of applied science. But the image of science as an ever-welcome bringer of good things was lost in 1945 in the ominous shadow of a mushroom cloud, never to be recovered. With the detonation of the first atom bomb, science outgrew its age of innocence. The bomb was the acknowledged offspring of an official union of science and government. It was evident even to the most optimistic that a highly dangerous power had been loosed upon the world. What was less evident, but soon to become so, was that science released other powers with capabilities for transforming the environment as thoroughly, if less dramatically.

Reforming Science in Policy: Forces for Change

Science per se was not the principal object of public misgiving during the 1960s. True, there were persons, often highly literate, who were disaffected with science as an enterprise. But the constructive criticisms of science, in which some scientists took a lead, were concerned with the development of its resources. These concerns were largely twofold: first, toward the kind of science that was receiving emphasis and support and, second, toward the ways in which science was being applied. Policy issues regarding weapons testing, nuclear fallout, and the hydrogen bomb were prominent in the initial controversies and involved serious considerations of environmental and health effects. These and other issues implied dissatisfaction with the existing public administration of science but not necessarily with science as a human enterprise.

Controversy over emphasis in science occurred not only among scientists, but also among government administrators, members of Congress, administrators of universities, and the information media. When, at the end of World War II, Vannevar Bush wrote *Science, the Endless Frontier,* there appeared to be a tacit understanding among persons prominent in government, business, and the information media that science was essentially physical science.[8] Its conventional subdivisions were physics, chemistry, astronomy, geology, and perhaps some aspects of biology. The social sciences were hardly regarded as serious sciences, although economics had a special place because it was perceived as being quantitative and dealt with "practical" affairs. Biologists differed as to what was science and what was mere nature study. Ecology was often relegated to the latter category.

Developments during World War II had a stimulating effect upon all of the conventional sciences and induced new types of investigation, for example, into computer technology, cybernetics, and systems behavior. The war not only produced technoscientific innovations such as the atom bomb, radar, and DDT but it led to enlarged capabilities for transportation, excavation, earthmoving, and construction that prepared the way for massive federal interventions in the environment in the postwar period. And perhaps of greatest long-term effect were advances in information technology and artificial intelligence using ever more sophisticated electronic techniques and computers. Advances in these fields opened doors to advancement in all of the sciences.

Early in the postwar period the fields of molecular biology and biochemistry expanded dramatically, and scientists tended to believe that the future of biology lay almost wholly in this direction. Ecology was regarded by many biologists as a dubious candidate for serious scientific status; indeed, some biologists sympathetic to the objectives of ecology preferred the term "environmental biology," responding to the opinion of some prestigious biologists that ecology was not a science. Nevertheless, connections between environmental events and biological effects were increasingly being discovered or suspected. Linkages between atomic fallout and genetic defects were widely accepted in scientific circles regardless of opinions regarding ecology.

The issue of what kind of science was SCIENCE came to a head in the establishment, funding, and development of the National Science Foundation following Vannevar Bush's call for a major national commitment to science. Although the National Science Foundation was established by Congress in 1950, leadership in its launching was almost exclusively confined to physical scientists. It was several years before the biological sciences, and even later the social sciences, found a place, even a grudging toleration. Congress played an important role in broadening the scope of the National Science Foundation. Early in the 1960s congressmen were beginning to sense a latent popular dissatisfaction with the heavily hardware-oriented application of science and technology. Why, it was asked, can we send men to the moon but are unable to clean up Lake

Erie? New emphases in funding for science began to be mandated by the Congress, and resulting programs, particularly in the area of environmental biology, added both respectability and resources for ecological research.

Official acquiescence in funding for environment-related research was certainly stimulated by the atomic fallout issue and by the controversies following publication of Rachel Carson's *Silent Spring,* in 1962. It may also have been nudged by a political perception of need for United States participation in international cooperative investigations such as the International Biological Program (1963–74). Even the often conservative National Academy of Sciences and the National Academy of Engineering were moved in 1967 to establish the Environmental Studies Board, following a recommendation from the president's Science Advisory Committee's 1965 report entitled *Restoring the Quality of Our Environment.* In 1969 the National Research Council sponsored a study conference on Research Strategies in the Social and Behavioral Sciences on Environmental Problems and Policies. During the late 1960s, five of the eight divisions of the National Research Council were engaged in studies relating to environmental pollution.

A parallel development of environmental concern was also occurring in the field of medicine. For many decades environmental aspects of health and disease had been largely ignored except in relation to specific illnesses carried by vectors (such as malaria) or resulting from bacterial contamination (food poisoning). Medical science concentrated upon techniques of diagnosis, immunization, and cure. Predisposing factors of an environmental character, however, began to attract interest among medical ecologists and public health administrators. In the 1960s the American Medical Association sponsored a series of environmental health congresses and environmental symposia were conducted by the National Sanitation Foundation. In 1964 in the *American Journal of Public Health,* George Rosen wrote of "the rediscovery of the environment." The National Institutes of Health, although adhering in the main to a conventional medical outlook, also reflected in the formation of new committees and some new programs the growing public and congressional concern with environmental influences upon health and disease.

And so during the 1960s a new field of interdisciplinary research and education began to take shape under the name of environmental science. Yet this development in science and education and the changes in public attitude that induced it were more than a reaction to the technoscientific excesses following World War II. The environmental-ecological movement had origins going back many decades before World War II. Emergence of an environmental emphasis in science in the 1960s was part of a larger expression of environmental concern.

Environmentalism as a political movement emerged as a consequence of a diversity of interests among which quality of the environment was a common denominator. Conspicuous areas of concern were public health, wildlife protection, outdoor recreation, urban and regional planning, land use and landscape planning, historic and cultural preservation, and energy policy. Coincident with these interests and concerns, a configuration of knowledge called environmental science converged from findings in a broad range of scientific fields. Although not a coherent science in the prevailing sense, the term "environmental science" helped to identify an increasing use of coordinated multidisciplinary research into problems of man-environment relationships. Thus it was a logical coincidence and certainly no accident that environmental science began to emerge at the time when people were becoming increasingly aware of the unwanted side effects of hitherto enthusiastically and uncritically welcomed technoscientific developments. Thus an environmental emphasis in science was both a cause and an effect of popular, and hence political, discontent.

The science-based public works and defense activities of the government during the 1940s laid a foundation for the exponential growth of big science, big government, and big technology in the postwar period. During the years of the Great Depression, the government launched a series of major environment-shaping activities in which technoscience played a significant role. Among them were the Tennessee Valley Authority, the Bonneville Dam, the Soil Conservation Service, and the Civilian Conservation Corps. The U.S. Army Corps of Engineers was charged to control floods, and the Bureau of Reclamation encouraged efforts to bring water to any land that could be irrigated in the rain-deficient West.

The sponsors of the Morrill Land Grant Act of 1862 would have been astonished could they have foreseen that they were the progenitors of the age of agribusiness. The marriage of agriculture and the mechanical arts in 1862 had produced within a century a mechanized agriculture fueled by petroleum and guided by the sciences of agronomy, chemistry, and plant genetics and by techniques of food processing and marketing applied to new energy-intensive, industrialized, high-production farming. The chemistry that made agribusiness possible was extended to forestry and to the lawns and gardens of a burgeoning population of American suburbanities. The sophisticated high-technology methods of scientific agriculture reinforced collectivizing trends, replacing the traditional family farm with the industrial farm, best epitomized in the Central Valley of California.

The first two decades following World War II were marked by a euphoric expansion of population and the economy. An explicit national commitment to growth existed, with little if any concern for its consequences inasmuch as they were generally believed to be unequivocally beneficial. It was an era of big plans, characterized by huge public projects in the West: massive transfers of water from northern to southern California, the multipurpose Garrison Diversion Unit in North Dakota, and mining, power, and irrigation enterprises in the Colorado basin of which the Central Arizona Project and Southwest Power were among the largest. Technocratic enthusiasts conceived NAWAPA, the North American Water and Power Alliance, which was to redistribute the water of western Canada not only throughout western but also central and eastern United States, and proposed the Rampart Dam on the Yukon, which would have flooded vast areas of waterfowl habitat in Alaska. The Public Works Committee of the House of Representatives and the Army Corps of Engineers thought big in projecting the Cross-Florida Barge Canal and the Tennessee-

Tombigbee Canal as well as a long list of lesser projects. And during the Eisenhower administration the Interstate Defense Highway System was launched—at its time the largest public works enterprise in history.

Thus at the end of the 1950s Americans could look with satisfaction (or so they then thought) upon the beneficence of providence and the new industrial state. Nuclear reactors would solve the energy problems of humanity for all time. DDT promised not only to wipe out the scourges of insect-carried diseases such as malaria but greatly to increase the yield of crops through the elimination of insect pests. Accompanying these benefits, biological science improved contraceptive technology, which among other benefits could ensure that America's resource base would not be overstressed through uncontrolled population increase.

Thus, at the beginning of the 1960s, the prospect for America's future could hardly seem brighter. Even the temporary setback in national self-confidence following the orbiting of the Russian satellite Sputnik and the early failures of Americans to match the achievement was rapidly overcome as Americans caught up with the Russians in space and President John Kennedy called for putting a man on the moon by the end of the decade.

In retrospect, the years 1968–69 appear to have been pivotal in a reorientation of science in public policy. Forces for change are often at work, unperceived beneath routine affairs. And ironically, the very triumph of an ideal or the achievement of a goal sometimes marks the birth of new and different purposes. On Christmas Eve of 1968, the Apollo IX astronauts, having circumnavigated the moon, first saw the entire earth from outer space, and their vision transmitted to earth and retransmitted from computerized receptors to the television screens of millions of Americans had a powerful symbolic effect upon the environmental movement that was then rapidly gaining momentum. The concept of the earth as a planetary spaceship, finite and fragile, became plausible in a way that never could have been achieved through literary expression, however eloquent. Eloquence was nevertheless inspired by the event, treating the vision of the whole earth in space as a parable for human behavior. Newly elected President Richard Nixon in his inaugural address, four weeks after Apollo IX, drew upon the poetry of Archibald MacLeish, who found a representation of the essential unity of humanity in that vision of the earth "as it truly is, small blue and beautiful in that eternal silence where it floats." The new president expressed what many others saw when he declared: "In that moment of surpassing technological triumph, men turned their thoughts toward home and humanity—seeing in that far perspective that man's destiny on earth is not divisible; telling us that however far we reach into the cosmos, our destiny lies not in the stars but on earth itself."[9]

Also in 1968 the General Assembly of the United Nations voted to convene a world conference on the human environment to meet in Stockholm in 1972, and in September of the same year, under the sponsorship of UNESCO and a number of associated international organizations, the Biosphere Conference met in Paris. But it was the vision of the blue earth against a black background of space as seen by the Apollo astronauts and transmitted to all mankind that gave emotional content to the expression "biosphere." And the whole earth as seen from outer space became a conceptual presence at the United Nations Conference on the Human Environment, symbolizing its motto, "only one Earth."

In the landing on the moon of July 1969, the postwar achievement of American technoscience reached its literal apex and, in December of the same year, the Congress of the United States passed the National Environmental Policy Act, which had as one of its major objectives the reformation of the uses of science in public policy and administration. Victory in space had served to accentuate human failure in custody and care of the earth. Hard science and technology in their conspicuous triumph in space were opening the way for a new and different emphasis in scientific research and application. The space scientists and engineers were, in effect, becoming involuntary midwives to an ecology-oriented environmental science of which some of them disapproved.

Chemistry and engineering in particular were targets of environmentalist and antiwar protest. Science as a profession was regarded by many persons on the liberal left as primarily serving military arrogance and corporate avarice. The seemingly endless war in Southeast Asia confirmed the fears of many people regarding the role of science in the service of the military-industrial complex. The charge of "ecocide" was leveled at the use of toxic defoliants by the American armed forces in Vietnam. Welfare advocates saw science as a competitor for funds. The Reverend Ralph Abernathy of the Southern Christian Leadership Conference criticized priorities represented by the collection of geological samples on the moon, saying that when a little black child asked for bread, government gave her a stone. No longer helped by the threat of Russian competition and unaided by an effective vote-getting political constituency, conventional science research and development began to lose public support. The environmental movement benefited only moderately from this change in the climate of opinion. It was more successful at obtaining a reordering of research priorities and an integrative use of multidisciplinary science than at obtaining new funds and institutional arrangements for environment-related research, a failure noted more fully in Chapter 5.

Public attitudes toward science, as toward almost anything else, have always been mixed. Although animus toward science per se grew, more fault was found with the way science and its technological applications were used. Reaction against "mismanaged" technoscience had already begun with publication of Rachel Carson's *Silent Spring* and Stewart Udall's *Quiet Crisis* (1963). President Lyndon Johnson had spoken of the dark side of technology and had called for a new conservation, which in essence was what the new environmental movement was to be. But no one more poignantly expressed the contrast between the magnificent achievement in space and the threat posed by the same technoscientific capability that made it possible than did Anne Lindbergh in "The Heron and the Astronaut," a poetic essay appearing in *Life Magazine* on 28 February 1969. "No one," she wrote, "will ever look at the earth in the same way. . . .

Through the eyes of the astronauts we have seen more clearly than ever before this precious earth-essence that must be preserved." If technoscience could place a man on the moon and return him to earth, why could not that same capability be employed to obtain the fruits of the earth without destroying the life-support system that made them possible?

Reforming Science in Policy: Directions of Change

The signing into law of the National Environmental Policy Act by President Richard Nixon on 1 January 1970 formally initiated a new era in the relationship between science, technology, and public policy in American government. But the initiation of new relationships was neither recognized nor conceded by many observers. Only time would tell whether priorities would really be reoriented and whether the new mandates would stick. Among both agencies and individuals, old priorities and old government-client relationships continued. After 1970, however, the traditional ways were increasingly on the defensive, notably in agriculture, highway construction, public works, and resource development. More than one engineer or technocrat expressed moral indignation when compelled to consider the birds and the bees and prepare an environmental impact statement. Early court cases, however, beginning with the Gillham Dam decisions (1971–72) and the Calvert Cliffs interpretation of NEPA by Judge J. Skelly Wright of the Circuit Court of Appeals for the District of Columbia (1971), served notice upon the agencies that tongue-in-cheek compliance would not do and that a strict observance of the environmental impact statement requirements of NEPA would be enforced in the federal courts.[10]

Yet a trend initiated is not a trend fully developed. A decade after the effective date of NEPA, resistance to the direction of policy that it mandated was less evident but continued in sometimes covert ways. For example, administrative officials have been alleged to "edit" scientific findings in the preparation of draft impact statements, ostensibly to make them more palatable to agency clients and interested politicians. "Splitting the difference" between the wishes of clients and the findings of scientists is sometimes called in the euphemistic language of politics "a balanced view." Compromise and the balancing of equities is the essence of politics and adjudication. But the quality of public policy depends upon the substance of the things that are balanced.

NEPA institutionalized a new direction in public policy that was to use science in an integrated interdisciplinary way to redress excessive weighting of agency decisions on the side of narrowly conceived economic and engineering considerations. But the emasculation of the Council on Environmental Quality in early 1981 as one of the first acts of the Reagan administration raised questions concerning the consequences of the council's weakened role in overseeing the NEPA process. Other signs of diminished official concern for the environment followed. The extent to which NEPA has been internalized in the various federal agencies was apparently to be tested.

Three successively overlapping phases of the science-government relationship following the watershed of the Civil War may be identified. First, before World War II, the relationship was symbolized by the word productivity; planned reduction of farm surpluses during the 1930s depression years was an expedient exception. The lead science agency and incubator for many science-related functions, some of which subsequently gained separate status, was the U.S. Department of Agriculture.[11] Its triangular relationship to farmers, to schools of agriculture and experiment stations in the states, and to the agricultural industry (equipment manufacturers, elevator owners, seed houses, meat packers, and the like) set a pattern for the encouragement of productivity that was enormously successful. Other areas in which a strong production-oriented government-client relationship encouraged the development of science were water power, forestry, and mining. In addition, government science was directed toward aiding production by providing information and standardization of quality through the Weather Bureau, the Food and Drug Administration, and the National Bureau of Standards, as well as through the inspection functions of the USDA.

In the second phase, after 1945, the emphasis in the government-science relationship shifted from material productivity to power and prestige. The uses of science were heavily directed toward the development of weapons, exploration of space, and, indirectly as a result of government needs, development activities in electronics and computers. New lead agencies in government science appeared, notably the Atomic Energy Commission and the National Aeronautics and Space Administration. A unified Department of Defense emerged as a major patron of the "hard" sciences.

Third, by 1970, a quarter century after the detonation of the first atom bomb, the relationship had begun to shift toward the use of science to improve the quality of life. The trend had been signalized by the Great Society program of Lyndon B. Johnson, emphasizing social welfare, civil rights, consumer protection, and environmental quality. It was a trend away from basic science toward applied science and, relative to budgetary commitments on behalf of "human needs," reflected a decline in public support for science. For example, the Johnson administration favored expanded health care delivery over biomedical research and in 1971 the National Science Foundation under pressure from the Congress established the Research Applied to National Needs (RANN) program. Another indication of the trend was an aroused public concern over possible violations of human rights in the course of scientific experiments, leading to establishment in 1974 of the National Commission for the Protection of Human Subjects of Biomedical and Behavioral Research.

Research to Meet National Needs

By 1980 it appeared to some observers that science was becoming a poor competitor for funds in the American version of an "entitlement society." Still impressively strong, American science and technology had slipped behind Western Europe and Japan in per capita investment and in significant areas of innovation. Discretionary spending for science seemed an inevitable target for budgetary retrenchment in the Reagan administration, caught between the promises of the president to increase the defense budget and the unwillingness of the Congress to jeopardize votes by reducing entitlements. Conventional "hard science" and engineering especially as related to defense and industrial productivity received administration support, but severe reduction of funding for social and ecological research was expected.

Only time will tell whether the new emphasis will be lasting. It would be unrealistic to assume that modifications of policy will not occur. But the dangers of inadequately considered or tunnel-vision uses of scientific knowledge and technology have now been experienced, documented, and publicized; they cannot safely be ignored. Imperfect as its understanding may be, the educated public in all modern countries is aware that the future may be jeopardized through degradation of the environment. Public reaction to episodes such as the incident at Three Mile Island, to discoveries at the Love Canal, and to numerous cave-ins, oil spills, and blowouts indicates that no matter how much people may resent the costs and inconveniences of environmental regulations and preventive measures, they will suffer their political discontents in preference to suffering the physical consequences of an unlivable environment.

No one can safely assert that science will not continue to be used in unwise and destructive ways. What has changed in the traditional government-science relationship is that public responsibility to anticipate the consequences of proposed applications of science and technology has obtained political acceptance. How this responsibility is discharged is a function of politics. Not all impacts of proposed government action upon the environment are amenable to assessment by scientific methods, and not all impacts result from applied science or technology. To factual uncertainties regarding the nature of impacts, there must be added differences in values—people seek different results from the environment.

NEPA represents an effort to redeploy the uses of science in agency planning and decisionmaking so as to identify and perhaps reduce uncertainties while affording opportunity for expression of values. But its drafters never believed that it could provide a procedural substitute for political judgment. Nevertheless, a public expectation has been created that the consequences of environmentally impacting action will be assessed before action is taken. Whatever modifications of the impact analysis process may be adopted, the general policy of prior comprehensive analysis seems certain to remain. This, at least, was the opinion of the federal planners and managers whom I interviewed in 1980 and 1981 in connection with a detailed study of the uses of science in the NEPA process.

Environmental impact analysis has been adopted pro forma in other nations, including an increasing number by governments in the so-called Third World. And through the United Nations system and the work of such international bodies as the International Council of Scientific Unions and the International Union for Conservation of Nature and Natural Resources, a global environmental ethic has been written into treaties, resolutions, and administrative practice. But only experience will tell us how deeply the ethic has penetrated and what its ultimate meaning will be.

It is still much too early to discount the pessimistic assessment attributed to Albert Schweitzer that "modern man has lost the ability to foresee or forestall, he will end by destroying the earth."[12] Yet NEPA is premised on the more hopeful assessment of human possibilities implicit in Schweitzer's more considered judgment when he wrote, "In my view no other destiny awaits mankind than that to which, through its mental and spiritual disposition, it prepares for itself. Therefore I do not believe that it will have to tread the road to ruin right to the end."[13]

3
Environmental Policy
as Administrative Reform

Exhortation has seldom been an effective instrument of political or moral reform. Yet, in as many as thirty-five environmental bills introduced into the 91st Congress, exhortation was almost the only means proposed for achieving a change of public policy to effect environmental protection. Senate Bill 1075 was distinctive in that it provided a means for promoting public policy through administrative reform instead of relying solely on declarations of moral purpose to be realized through unenforceable admonishments. Although not generally perceived at the time, one effect of the National Environmental Policy Act of 1969 was to supplement the federal Administrative Procedure Act of 1946 (APA) and, through regulations subsequently issued by the CEQ and the agencies, to place the environmental impact statement process under the strictures laid down by the courts for informal rulemaking under provisions of APA.

A Strategy for Reform

The National Environmental Policy Act answered a problem of legislative strategy: how to legislate effectively in an area of conceptual novelty where constitutional authority and jurisdictional boundaries were unclear.

Members of the 90th and 91st Congresses recognized an inchoate but persistent public demand for national action to arrest the deterioration of the American environment. Unlike most reform movements with which congressmen were familiar, however, public demand during the 1960s that "something be done about the environment" was seldom accompanied by specific proposals for legislation. In this respect, the National Environmental Policy Act was a political anomaly. It was not promoted by lobbyists, and although supported by the mainline conservation organizations, was not a product of their draftsmen. It developed its constituency after rather than before enactment, although in its drafting congressional committee staffs consulted extensively with groups interested in environmental legislation.

In July 1968 the Senate Committee on Interior and Insular Affairs and the House Committee on Science and Astronautics cosponsored a colloquium at the Capitol in which a broad spectrum of interests was represented.[1] The House-Senate colloquium was in effect an invitational public hearing to consider the need for a national policy for the environment. The committee staffs made serious efforts to involve a representative sample of Americans with interests and knowledge relative to a national environmental policy. It was not a hearing orchestrated by conservationists or environmentalists, although persons representing traditional conservation interests were present. The term "environmentalist" had not yet come into common usage, but NEPA and the larger body of environmental legislation enacted in the late 1960s and early 1970s helped create the constituency that would be called environmentalist. Subsequently, indiscriminate use of this term in the news media deprived it of descriptive value.

The drafting of NEPA was primarily the work of the staff of the Senate Committee on Interior and Insular Affairs with the assistance of the committee's own consultants and staff from the Congressional Research Service with inputs from the Federal Council for Science and Technology and the National Research Council. It should not be inferred that the mainline conservation organizations had no input into the drafting. They were consulted, but their views had long been in the public domain as part of the literature and the testimony relating to conservation policies in general and to specific legislative proposals. Among the more relevant of the latter was the Ecological Research and Survey Bill introduced into the Senate in 1965 by Senator Gaylord Nelson of Wisconsin, from which much of the substance of Title II of NEPA was drawn.[2]

After detailed but relatively minor compromises during drafting and intercommittee negotiations, NEPA emerged as a remarkably coherent piece of policy legislation. The form of the act may in part be attributed to the fact that Congress responded to a perceived public interest in a way idealists might think it should respond. It was not pressured by militant interest groups threatening reprisals if legislation were not enacted to serve their particular objectives. As compared with other statutes relating to environmental protection, NEPA was phrased at a high level of generality, but this was appropriate to a "policy act" intended to declare broad national goals and to provide procedural guidelines toward their attainment, applicable to all agencies throughout the wide range of the federal service. Nevertheless, the act was specific in important particulars, not the least of which was the action-forcing provision—one of the critical elements in the strategy of obtaining an effective piece of legislation.

The fundamental element of the strategy, however, was to approach a national policy for the environment through an avenue in which the Congress had unquestionable authority: to restate the priorities and to redirect the emphasis of the federal administrative agencies. Whatever the missions and responsibilities of the agencies, the Congress had the authority to specify that they be administered in the public interest. Taking care to see that the American environment was not unduly impaired in the course of federal administration was clearly in line with protection of the public interest.

This strategy problem of legislating for the environment was solved in the following manner. After declaring the elements of a national policy for the environment in Section 101 of NEPA, the Congress in subsequent sections specified procedures to ensure that impacts of major federal actions on the environment were fully considered. This was accomplished primarily through Section 102, which mandated a systematic, inter-disciplinary method of planning and called for integrated use of the natural and social sciences and the environmental de-sign arts. In addition, the agencies were required to take measures to incorporate nonquantified considerations in their policymaking. Uncertain of presidential support for the mea-sure and certain of bureaucratic resistance, the drafters de-vised an action-forcing provision in the five-point environmen-tal impact statement requirement.

This provision, Section 102(2)(c) of NEPA is, in effect al-though not in legal fact, a supplement to the Administrative Procedure Act. In the words of Judge J. Skelly Wright, it set a "strict standard of compliance" for the federal agencies, "a standard which must be rigorously enforced by the reviewing courts."[3] And NEPA was distinguished from all other environ-mental policy proposals introduced into the 90th and 91st Congresses by specification of a procedure which unfortunately many persons have subsequently confused with the act itself. Nevertheless, it is the procedure that gives the act its vitality and justifies our regarding it as a major piece of administrative reform.

Administrative Reform through Science

NEPA has not been the only legislation that requires admin-istrative agencies to conform to scientific procedures and evidence. Basic legislation for the Forest Service, the Bureau of Land Management, the Nuclear Regulatory Commission, and the Food and Drug Administration imposes procedural and evidentiary uses of science. But NEPA is distinctive in invoking science in the broadest sense to guide the way in which science is to be used. The environmental impact statement in itself is not a scientific document, nor is environmental impact analysis necessarily a scientific procedure. Nevertheless, to achieve its purposes such analysis must use scientific information and methods. It is an administrative procedure intended to force administrative agencies to consider the goals of NEPA in plan-

ning and decisionmaking for which a significant environmen
tal impact is anticipated. The impact statement required
under Section 102(2)(c) is an instrument for enforcing application of the systematic interdisciplinary science mandated under Section 102(2)(a) to management decisions, many of which
are ostensibly based upon scientific knowledge.

NEPA did not introduce science into administrative planning and decisionmaking. Some aspect of science has played a
significant role in nearly every agency and area of public policy.
The uses of science in policy have been particularly noticeable
in the great resource management agencies such as the Corps
of Engineers, the Bureau of Reclamation (or Water and Power
Resources Service), the Forest Service, the Bureau of Land
Management, the Soil Conservation Service, and the Fish and
Wildlife Service, among others.

The drafters of NEPA were well informed about the ways the
federal agencies used science. They had consulted extensively
with staff members of the Federal Council of Science and
Technology as well as with personnel in the National Academy
of Sciences, the National Research Council, the Smithsonian
Institution, the Environment and Resources Division of the
Congressional Research Service, and the National Institutes of
Health. They had observed the experience of an Office of
Ecology in the Department of the Interior. Thus, contrary to
criticisms of NEPA by those whose reading of the statute
appears to have been superficial, the drafters did not assume
that there was somewhere in each agency an individual om-
nicompetent decisionmaker. Nor did they assume that scientific analysis alone was sufficient to assess the full impact of
agency action upon the environment. It was not the function of
this "policy act" to prescribe a predetermined process or outcome of public decisionmaking. Rather, in the light of declared
national objectives, the act required that administrative action
be preceded by consideration of its possible environmental
consequences.

The agencies had used science in many different ways, and
they had tended consistently to invoke it in defense of their
policies in public hearings and in congressional testimony. But

dequacy of the science or the correctness of tions were seldom possible until after the is had been made. Thus the way the agencies , science was not often challenged or challenged iy. Before the Freedom of Information Act of 1966 and iberalization of the rules of the courts regarding class iction suits, it was difficult to question the uses of science by the federal agencies. Public hearings had been notoriously ineffective for challenging decisions that had probably already been made or plans that had already been approved and were at the point of execution.

As with many innovations in politics, this challenge to official uses of science emerged through a process of convergence. The effectiveness of the NEPA process must be attributed in significant part to events coincident with it. Among these, as previously noted, was the rise of an environmental awareness in the public health movement and public concern over air and water pollution, nuclear fallout, pesticides, food additives, and diminishing wildlife.

A growing restiveness with official secrecy and bureaucratic reticence in sharing information with the public had led to the Freedom of Information Act and was also expressed through the development of public interest law firms. Several of these, for example, the Natural Resources Defense Council, the Environmental Defense Fund, and the Environmental Law Institute, focused specifically on resource, conservation, and environmental issues.

Two closely linked developments of political significance were the rise of a new affluent middle class in the post–World War II period and a growing public interest, especially within this middle class, in outdoor recreation and environmental amenities. A relatively young, mobile, family-forming postwar generation with paid vacations and the means to travel began to make demands upon state and national parks and recreation areas that found official response in the Outdoor Recreation Resources Review Commission established in 1958. An official result was the establishment in 1962 of the Bureau of Outdoor Recreation in the Department of the Interior.

Another indication of the emergence of environmental amenity values on the part of a relatively young and affluent population was the increase in membership in the mainline conservation and outdoor recreation organizations and the establishment of new organizations devoted to environmental protection. Organizations such as the Sierra Club, the National Audubon Society, and the Wilderness Society had once been regarded with benign unconcern by the Corps of Engineers, the Forest Service, and the Bureau of Reclamation. But throughout the 1960s the influence of the environmental groups grew rapidly, and they began to win impressive victories such as stopping Rampart Dam and saving the Dinosaur National Monument. Especially after NEPA, the agencies were compelled to take these organizations more seriously as the EIS provided a new means to call the government to account.

These volunteer citizen groups now discovered that their memberships were sufficiently numerous to bring substantial amounts of money into their treasuries. When public officials honestly pursue their understanding of the public interest, it may be wrong to say that "money talks," but it is surely right to observe that it can powerfully facilitate communication. The environmental action groups attracted growing numbers of skilled communicators among an increasing membership active in business and professional life. The conservation groups could no longer be regarded as composed primarily of children and little old ladies in tennis shoes. A consequence of this development was that conservation organizations could now often afford to employ first-class lawyers, economists, ecologists, and systems analysts. They could produce talent capable of trumping a Corps of Engineers cost-benefit analysis. Thus, whereas in the pre-NEPA controversies science had been almost wholly at the service of government and business, the balance was now more even. Areas of policy were enlarged in which scientists could challenge scientists with respect to the appropriateness and adequacy of the information upon which proposed action was based. It now became feasible to question official interpretations of data.

Contradictory invocations of science occurred regularly in

hearings and litigations regarding policies of the Food and Drug Administration, the Atomic Energy Commission, and the Fish and Wildlife Service, for example. But in these cases the protests against official policy were largely over interpretations of fact and did not effectively change the procedures or the inputs employed in official planning or decisionmaking. Scientists representing the chemical and pharmaceutical industries frequently challenged the scientific conclusions of government scientists on matters at issue, but these adversary procedures had no way of restructuring the analytic methods of the agencies or of altering the informational inputs into agency decisions or proposed regulations.

NEPA did not make public administration as a political process more scientific, but it did make administrative action vulnerable to public protest and judicial review if scientific information was not used in legally defensible ways consistent with the mandates and goals of the act. A large part of the action of federal agencies both directly and indirectly had an impact upon the environment, and it was the intent of the drafters of NEPA to use science to increase the probability that this impact would not be adverse.

Structuring Policy Change

Enactment of NEPA meant that each agency had new priorities to consider and a new function to perform—environmental impact analysis possibly leading to a fully developed environmental impact statement. Short of a complete EIS, an environmental assessment would be required if the impact, although not major, were nevertheless significant. Agencies were compelled to make facilitating administrative adjustments to meet the environmental impact statement requirement. First, the agencies faced an organizational task in accommodating the EIS function to existing structures and procedures. Second, NEPA partly implied and partly mandated new procedures in agency planning and decisionmaking which in fact constituted administrative procedural reform.

Third, new personnel needs were encountered. Few agencies had personnel ready to undertake environmental impact analysis as required by NEPA, and those who had the basis of such competence almost invariably required reorientation or training. Fourth, and immediately apparent to the agencies, were the budgetary requirements of the EIS procedure. Fifth, NEPA added a new public relations dimension to administrative activities, primarily through the stipulation that the public could have access to and comment on draft impact statements and that those comments would remain as a part of the permanent record of the statement through its several stages.

The EIS provision has been appropriately described as action-forcing, but the substance of action to be forced is described in other portions of NEPA. Proceeding on the assumption that administrative reform was essential to policy change and further assuming that the way science was used was critical to the achievement of policy goals, the drafters of NEPA sought to reform administration by changing the ways scientific knowledge and method were used. To the extent that agencies used science in decisionmaking, there tended to be a set of reciprocal relationships between an agency's goal or mission, organizational structure, and uses of science. The ways agencies used science appeared to be inherent in the ways their missions were structured, but those structures appeared in part to be influenced by the areas of science that agencies characteristically used.

Agencies relying on the physical sciences and engineering for execution of their missions learned only indirectly, if at all, what biological and social effects their projects produced. Their organizational structure made no provision for competence outside of their traditional areas of expertise. NEPA expanded their planning horizons directly through Section 102(2)(a), which required a systematic interdisciplinary use of the sciences including the natural and social sciences and environmental design arts; through 102(2)(b), which required consideration of unquantified values; through Section 102(2)(h), which required the use of ecological information; and indirectly through the environmental impact statement requirement of Section 102(2)(c).

The specific impact of NEPA on administrative organization and procedure within the federal government occurred on two levels. The first, or oversight level, was occupied by the Council on Environmental Quality and for certain purposes by the Environmental Protection Agency. Under NEPA the CEQ was established in the Executive Office of the President but with jurisdiction that extended to other federal agencies, not merely those under the direct authority of the president. The second level was of course that of the individual federal departments and agencies. Beyond the federal government, NEPA has influenced administrative policy, structure, and procedure among the fifty states as well as in a number of national governments and international organizations abroad.

Title II of NEPA charges the CEQ with both coordinative and promotional responsibilities. In practice, neither the president nor the Congress has allowed full exercise of this statutory function. Neither the executive nor the legislative branch has been inclined to encourage CEQ intervention in agency policy- and decisionmaking, and the Congress has never been willing to appropriate funds sufficient to permit the CEQ to carry out its promotional mandate. Anticipation of this presidential-congressional diffidence caused the drafters of NEPA to provide for its enforcement through judicial review, independent of initiatives by the so-called political branches of the government.

Although President Richard Nixon appointed a strong CEQ and gave it unpredicted support before the distractions that led to his resignation, it was not until the Carter administration that the oversight role of the CEQ was clarified and reinforced by Executive Order 11991 (24 May 1977), which vested in the council the authority to issue regulations with the force of law. And it was by Executive Order 12114 (9 January 1979) that President Carter clarified the application of the National Environmental Policy Act to the activities of the United States overseas, to the extraterritorial functions of the Defense Department and the Department of State in particular.

The election of Ronald Reagan to the presidency in 1980 brought into power, for the first time in the history of NEPA, an administration that regarded the environmental concerns of the previous decade as excessive and believed that reasonable environmental goals had been attained and further initiatives were unnecessary. The survival of the CEQ as an effective instrument of environmental oversight was uncertain although, because it was a statutory agency, Congress would have to consent to its abolition. The priorities of presidents have been known to change during their tenure of office, but at the end of Reagan's first year in office, it appeared that the CEQ might experience an indefinite period of suspended animation.

The other administrative oversight agency, the Environmental Protection Agency, was established by Reorganization Plan 3 of 1970, initially combining a number of separately administered ongoing regulatory functions. These functions involved some measure of scientific research, monitoring, and standard-setting in relation to air and water quality, pesticide control, and radiation protection. Functions relating to noise abatement, toxic substances, and land use were subsequently added. The reorganization of pollution control functions was directly influenced by scientific information. The original categorical organization of pollution control showed a limited understanding of the origins and interactions of environmental pollutants. Their passage from air to water to soil and through organisms implied that effective control must address the phenomenon as a whole, and this was what the integration of the pollution control functions under the EPA was designed to do.

Unfortunately, it appears easier to solve problems by reorganization than by time-consuming, budget-demanding research. The theory of integrated pollution control was sound, but the science to implement it has often been shaky. Even EPA's Science Advisory Board has criticized the scientific basis for many EPA standards which, significantly, have been drafted and administered primarily by lawyers. NEPA and its associated laws and regulations have stimulated scientific research, which in time may provide a more adequate basis for policy. Meanwhile, the more appropriate complaint to be made regarding EPA is not inadequate science but unrealistic regulation.

The primary oversight function of EPA with regard to NEPA derives from Section 309 of the Clean Air Act, which requires that it review and comment on environmental impact statements of all federal agencies. Section 309b of this act authorizes EPA referral to the CEQ in cases of determination by the administrator of EPA that the "legislation, action, or regulation is unsatisfactory from the standpoint of public health or welfare or environmental quality." The comments of EPA and the referral by the administrator become matters of public record. Although CEQ and presidential action pursuant to this referral are by law discretionary, the public disclosure involved may be prejudicial to an agency's reputation or policy strategy and may open the way to legal action on the part of objecting citizens.

The NEPA authorization of the CEQ "to conduct investigations, studies, surveys, research, and analyses" was transferred to the EPA under Reorganization Plan 3 reflecting the theory that as a staff agency, advisory to the president, the CEQ should not perform line or operating functions. This NEPA function has never been effectively performed by the EPA, although in 1971 an Environmental Studies Division (ESD) began an examination and comprehensive analysis of long-range problems relating to the environment.

This effort in EPA was not sustained, however. Commenting on the apparent inability of the government to effectuate the research needed to fulfill NEPA goals, Peter W. House, who headed the ESD effort, suggests that "substantial changes will have to be made in the policymaking structure to seriously include comprehensive analyses. These changes will have to be permanent throughout the whole institutional system, from the way we are taught to look at a problem to the way we carry out our policies."[4]

Experience confirms this conclusion and indicates the importance of where and how a high-level oversight and review function is located, which in turn raises a more fundamental question of political philosophy. Are the policies and goals enunciated in NEPA significant enough to justify extraordinary attention at the presidential level? Or are they now merely among the ordinary responsibilities of government singled out temporarily for special attention as a consequence of the wave of environmental consciousness that engulfed the nation in the 1960s and 1970s?

This latter view is that of many organizational and political conservatives. Some would perhaps agree with former White House staffer John C. Whitaker that "by 1976 CEQ had probably passed the zenith of its influence on the Executive Office of the President, primarily because so much had been accomplished that the institution had tended to work itself out of a job." In Whitaker's opinion, "a time will come, probably by 1980, when CEQ should cease to exist. By then, if the job has been well done, protection of the environment will be built into federal decisionmaking and the executive branch will not need an environmental watchdog."[5]

In my view, Whitaker underestimated the need for continuing surveillance of the nation's environmental problems beyond the scope of individual agency concerns. Internalization of environmental responsibility in the agencies was indeed a major objective of NEPA and one toward which notable progress appears to have been made. But the commitment to environmental quality and protection has dimensions that Whitaker appears to have overlooked. A coordinative oversight function was seen by many advocates of an environmental council before NEPA was enacted, and agency responsibility, however well intended, could not provide for this need. It is suggestive of the mind-set and value priorities of persons who say that CEQ's job has been accomplished that none, to my knowledge, has also advocated abolishing the Council of Economic Advisors or relegating it to the Department of the Treasury.

In interviews with environmental and planning personnel in the Bureau of Land Management, the Forest Service, and the Corps of Engineers I have been told that although an environmental concern had been internalized within the agency, the oversight role of the CEQ had been helpful in resolving differences of interpretation and assisting in novel situations in the application of NEPA and its regulations. Nowhere did agency planners or environmental analysts agree that the CEQ had worked itself out of a job and had become redundant. The dispensability of the CEQ, as of many other agencies of government, is a matter of value judgment.

During the four years of the Carter administration, development of regulations for implementing the procedural provisions of NEPA marked a significant advance in administrative reform; subsequently, the *Global 2000* report exemplified, at least in principle, the comprehensive overview function that the CEQ was intended to perform. Even in retrospect it may be too early to make a fair assessment of the administration of NEPA under Jimmy Carter. As with many other aspects of his policies, the record of his presidency was contradictory. Ostensibly committed to NEPA objectives, he nevertheless endorsed one of the most environmentally damaging proposals in a decade—the land-based mobile MX missile system. His budget cutting impaired the effectiveness of the CEQ, and he failed to capitalize politically on the important environmental accomplishments of his administration.

Time will be required to assess the depth and durability of the Reagan reaction of 1981. Will it prove to be more rhetoric than substance? Will President Reagan play a Louis XVIII role of monarchial reaction to what Max Nicholson has called "the environmental revolution"?[6] If commitment to NEPA goals has been built into the expectations of the federal agencies, the effects of the reaction may be largely superficial, but only time will tell.

It is seldom possible to penetrate behind a belief into its psychological origin, but in efforts to understand political ideologies it is often instructive to try. The apprehension which some conventionally well-informed persons have shown toward the environmental protection movement and NEPA in particular may reveal a basic distaste for bureaucratic decisionmaking, claiming authenticity in the name of science. Although NEPA was intended to counteract arbitrary and single-vision uses of science in policy, these uses have not been so perceived by those sectors of the public eager to get on with building highways, dams, and irrigation systems and with maximizing the commercial yield from farms, mines, and forests. On the contrary, some development-minded persons see retention of wilderness areas, protection of endangered species, and historic preservation as arbitrary, single-purpose policies, denying the broad diversity of public interests. Environmental policy is politics, and science, being instrumental to policy ends, is perceived differently from differing political viewpoints. Circumstantial evidence suggests that the reluctance of the Congress and the president to support comprehensive ecological surveillance and research reflects, at least in part, a belief that too much scientific knowledge could be politically unwelcome. It could make political compromise more difficult.

It may seem contradictory to fault environmental regulations and impact assessment as deficient in scientific substance and method and simultaneously to oppose funding the research necessary to overcome these deficiencies. Yet this is the position taken by many opponents of environmental protection measures. If the consequences of scientific inquiry are foreseen to limit growth, to foreclose development opportunities, and to impose new and unfamiliar requirements for farming, manufacturing, and waste disposal, the following position is logical: present environmental findings and controls are faulty because their science base is flawed—but further investment in environmental science is undesirable because it would only lead to increased burdens on the economy. Environmental conditions, moreover, are not nearly as bad as alleged and are getting better in spite of—not because of—bureaucratic interference. And anyway, some environmental degradation is a small price to pay for jobs and the benefits of modern industrial society. So runs the argument.

When science has come up with the "wrong" answers to problems for which expedient solutions are sought, it has not been popular, especially not with politicians. Peter House observes that at the higher policy levels in government "there is little real desire to know enough to make holistic decisions."[7] Nor would there be reason to know, unless—and this may be the heart of the matter—there was the intention to act upon the knowledge. To do this would be to plan and to act holistically—a prospect especially abhorrent to libertarians, many economists, political conservatives, and "practical" politicians.

If the CEQ had vigorously followed up on the policy implications of the *Global 2000* report, its findings and recommendations could easily have jeopardized policy options favored by many growth-and-development-minded congressmen and administrators. Effective use of its mandate under Title II of NEPA could have cast the CEQ in the role of a national environmental planning body. Thus the CEQ may have been perceived as a return of the New Deal National Resources Planning Board. Yet contrary to what might have been expected, the Reagan administration acquiesced in a CEQ-interagency committee analysis of the *Global 2000* report. Moreover the president publicly commended the International Union for Conservation of Nature and Natural Resources on its world conservation strategy, an effort paralleling *Global 2000*.

At the agency level, the structural problem presented by NEPA has been very different. Here new responsibilities and a new procedure had to be accommodated within existing operating organizations. To add or to integrate was the question confronting the federal agencies in building the new NEPA requirements onto or into their organizational structures. How the agencies have answered this question has depended largely upon three considerations: first, how the act was interpreted by agency administrators; second, the nature of the agency's mission as perceived by agency personnel and clients; and third, the organizational structure of the agency.

In the big natural resource management agencies within the Department of Agriculture, the Department of the Interior, and the Corps of Engineers, environmental impact analysis required access to scientific information and expertise that was partially consistent with the agencies' primary missions. Customary recourse to science did not necessarily make these agencies more responsive to NEPA but facilitated the use of science in the EIS when it did occur. In many of the other agencies, however, notably in the Department of Housing and

Urban Development, the Federal Aviation Agency, and the Agency for International Development, the environmental considerations that NEPA mandated were alien to agency tradition and to perceived responsibilities. Some, like the Atomic Energy Commission and the defense agencies (other than the Corps of Engineers), had assessed certain environmental impacts of their operations but not for the purpose of balancing environmental quality and mission objectives in their decision processes. These agencies tended to regard environmental impact statements as time-wasting nuisances, and agency administrators were hard put to see how the environmental impact assessment function could be integrated into the agencies' normal procedures. If the organizational response were guided by the intent of NEPA, the answer should have been readily apparent: integration with agency planning capabilities. In fact, the organizational response was determined in each agency by considerations of tradition, existing structure, and personnel—in brief, by intra-agency politics.

The exact mix of factors influencing each agency's individual response to the NEPA mandate is probably not ascertainable and in any case not highly significant here. Budgetary considerations and congenital bureaucratic aversion to reorganization may have been influential in some cases, although weighting the relevant factors is a matter of judgment and in any case would not be amenable to anything that could be called "proof." The obvious implications of the foregoing remarks is that most agencies opted for the "add on" answer to the need for administrative reorganization. The least disturbing organizational solution to coping with the NEPA process was to add an environmental office. This was the structural response that most agencies could make with the least amount of disruption over the shortest period of time. And with the sudden need to respond operationally to the new NEPA process with new and sometimes unfamiliar science specialists, the solution made sense.

The implication of Section 102 of NEPA should have been clear. Theoretically, the new NEPA requirements should, at the outset, have been built into the existing structure for policy planning and programming and the structure modified to accommodate the look-before-leaping mandate of NEPA. But in addition to the aforementioned considerations, agencies may have perceived a symbolic value in creating an office explicitly for the purpose of environmental analysis, rather than to have obscured this function by incorporating it in existing arrangements for agency planning. Other factors that resist empirical testing were by common knowledge often present in agency considerations. One of these was the resistance of "old-line" civil servants to "newfangled" environmental impact analysis or environmental impact considerations. Another was a hope that isolation of environmental functions from agency decision processes would reduce the risk of disruption of routine agency planning by environmental lawsuits and adverse judgments relating to environmental impact statements.

Such considerations may have influenced the large resource management agencies to create separate hierarchies of environmental offices parallel to the agency planning divisions. Effective integration of the new environmental impact analysis function with established agency planning procedures and personnel required time. In testimony before a House of Representatives Oversight Committee in 1976, George L. Turcott, associate director of the Bureau of Land Management (BLM), observed the reluctance of old "hands-on" managers out on the rangelands administered by BLM to accept the new "scientific" approach to decisionmaking on such matters as the issuance of grazing permits. The regional organization of the BLM by states and the long-standing interpersonal relationships between its field personnel and their major resource clients added to the probability that to rely upon existing agency structure for implementing NEPA would be to condemn the new procedures to no more than symbolic observance.

The Corps of Engineers, with a different tradition and organizational structure, nevertheless arrived at a generally similar solution to the challenge of the NEPA process. The corps, being preeminently a planning agency and traditionally dealing with environmental factors although not in NEPA terms, found it easier to build environmental analysis into its regular structure. Given the environment-shaping functions of the Civil Works division of the Corps of Engineers, the incorporation of environment analysis in the regular planning activities was not difficult to justify. Even so, functional separation of environmental studies from general planning activities was customary.

A factor of additional significance in the Civil Works division would appear to have been the paramilitary character of the agency as a whole; that is, although the overwhelming number of the planners in the Civil Works division of the corps are civilians, the structure of the corps as an integral part of the Department of the Army is essentially authoritative and military. Thus, at least in principle, orders from headquarters are carried through the divisional offices to the district offices of the corps, and a higher degree of internal coherence exists than in some of the essentially civilian agencies. Nevertheless, the corps operationally is highly decentralized at the district level. Responsiveness to general policy directives from the chief's office is in practice adjusted to accommodate responsiveness to local political pressures. In recent years, however, some of these pressures have been pro-environmental at times, counterbalancing the traditional development-minded corps clientele.

For whatever reasons, the corps appears to have adapted organizationally and operationally to NEPA requirements more readily than did other agencies. It reversed a long practice of policy exclusiveness, and in some districts citizen participation in "open planning" was invited. Daniel A. Mazmanian and Jeanne Nienaber conclude that the corps commitment to open planning diminished somewhat with experience.[8] Nevertheless, NEPA did induce administrative changes in the corps that appear to have endured.

Budget, Personnel, and Procedure

Although the agencies do not appear to have been notably alert to the implications of Senate Bill 1075 in the course of its

enactment, they became audibly concerned once the bill became serious law. But agency inquiry to Senator Jackson and
the Interior Committee regarding additional funds to meet the
NEPA requirements proved disappointing. The answer from
the Senate was to reorient priorities and reallocate money.

This reply was consistent with the intent of the law, but it
was not the answer the agencies wanted. They preferred to add
the costs incurred onto existing budgets. Moreover, alleged
costs of compliance with NEPA mandates might conveniently
cover costs more appropriately charged to program planning,
as appears to have been the case with the Bureau of Land
Management's allocation of the cost of environmental impact
studies pursuant to issuance of grazing permits.[9] In this way,
an agency could avoid charges of excessive costs of planning
through the alibi of the burdensome EISs laid upon it by the
requirements of NEPA as interpreted by the courts. The BLM
grazing permit episode may be seen in retrospect as one of
many situations that agencies encountered in the early years of
NEPA in joining the new environmental requirements to previously established planning procedures. By the beginning of
the 1980s the integration of environmental analysis with program and project planning appears to have been accomplished,
at least in the major resource management agencies.

Both the Senate Interior Committee and agency positions on
the effective use of science in policy were logical. Reorientation
of agency priorities was a goal of NEPA, and to build the EIS
procedure into agency planning and decisionmaking was a
means to this end. If the agencies had been doing an adequate
job of planning before taking action, and had budgeted accordingly, Senator Jackson's position would have been more tenable.
As it was, few agencies had previously planned in a manner
adequate to meet the Section 102 mandate of NEPA. They did
need more money, which in time many of them obtained. But
here, as in other aspects of NEPA, the Congress and the president preferred inexpensive symbolism to effective action that
cost money.

There is a French saying that "qui veut le fin, veut les
moyens" (he who wills the end wills the means). But this

aphorism found an apparent exception in congressional appropriations pursuant to the purposes of the National Environmental Policy Act. As noted, budget allocations for the EIS process were increased slowly and grudgingly. The CEQ was never adequately funded, and its budget, meager in relation to its responsibilities, was reduced when presidents cut spending across the board in the Executive Office to set an example for the agencies.

If the Congress really willed the reorientation of agency priorities that NEPA declared, it would have been logical to provide funds and authorization for reeducation and training of agency personnel having significant environmental responsibilities. In fact, no major effort was made in this direction. In time, practical necessity compelled the agencies, especially those involved in natural resource management, to institute measures for upgrading the capability of their employees to carry out the NEPA mandates.

The significance of this record of reluctant implementation by the Congress of its own declared policy is that the logic inherent in the language of NEPA ultimately forced legislative and administrative action to provide the budgets and personnel that were necessary to the attainment of NEPA goals. Whether this "muddling through" method cost less and achieved more in the long run is a moot point. Implementation of as novel a piece of legislation as NEPA required a learning process and experimentation. The United States was first among nations to attempt so extensively to modify an understandable inclination of bureaucracy to place mission goals before environmental consequences. In attempting this modification, the Congress was indirectly inviting exposure of its own traditional inclination toward "pork barrel," "logrolling" public works appropriations and toward economic development generally in preference to environmental quality. But the capacity of the Congress for inconsistency from any perspective but its own cannot be overestimated. NEPA has never induced a conspicuous show of self-denial or environmental conscientiousness among congressmen. It has made it less practical for them to urge projects so environmentally "bad" that exposure through the NEPA process would almost certainly cause their demise.

Before NEPA, exposing harmful environmental consequences, although not impossible, was not easy. Bringing to public notice the effects of big projects such as the Rampart Dam was expensive but feasible; more difficult to expose were less dramatic projects that slipped through the authorization process with little notice. Agency plans were open to scrutiny under the Freedom of Information Act only if somebody asked. The NEPA contribution was to open the analysis of environmental consequences to involuntary public exposure and to democratize the process for presenting conflicting claims regarding the relevance and adequacy of scientific knowledge. Under the EIS requirement any part of the public was entitled to press for consideration of additional evidence or overlooked facts. The desired outcome of this public involvement in administrative action was a more sensitive and complex balancing of the values inherent in available alternatives. It might be argued that this process at its best provided a practical way to approximate that elusive goal of discovering the "public interest."

Was it the combination of a procedural requirement with a substantive emphasis that made the National Environmental Policy Act confusing to so many of the legal counsel to the federal agencies and exasperating to many agency administrative personnel and their clients? Because of the EIS, agency counsel and the attorneys of agency clients appeared initially to have focused upon the procedural aspects of NEPA to the neglect of its substantive implications. And because the courts soon interpreted "major Federal actions," as stated in Section 102(2)(c), to include such client-related activities as contracting, licensing, and permitting, and the agencies accordingly required their clients to assist in the preparation of the environmental impact statements, the inference was drawn that NEPA was a new kind of regulation, thrust upon an already overburdened private economy. Even after a decade of experience with NEPA it has not been clear to all who should have known better that NEPA was not a lawyer's law but a policymaker's law. And the difference between an act that is primarily policy shaping in intent and one that is primarily regulatory apparently remains unclear to persons who still decry the unreasonable burden that environmental impact analysis imposes upon government and the private sector.

In NEPA the distinction is not wholly clear because although intended primarily to declare a national purpose (policy) the act does involve the regulation of agency planning and decisionmaking pursuant to that purpose. Internal regulations relating to environmental impact analysis are indirectly applied to the private sector to the extent that agency clients are required to participate in the EIS process for projects initiated outside the federal government. Nevertheless, NEPA, unlike the clean air and water laws, is not primarily concerned with regulating behavior in detail. Policy is implicit in all regulations, but the relative importance of broad policy goals as against legal requirements and technical specifications is much greater in NEPA than, for example, in pollution control measures. NEPA properly interpreted is focused primarily upon ends and, except for the EIS to certify that these ends have been observed, leaves their implementation to agency discretion.

Has NEPA been an effective instrument of administrative reform? Relative to its novelty and to other statutes, the answer today appears to be yes. In 1975, when the Congressional Research Service sponsored a workshop on NEPA, the answer was not so certain. Perhaps a majority of commentators during NEPA's early years doubted that its goals could be achieved. But after a decade of experience and with regulations supplementing the statute and correcting earlier misapplications, the case for its effectiveness is stronger. Even as early as 1974 a law review commentator declared, "It is hard to dismiss as ineffectual a statute which the Corps of Engineers says caused it to drop 24 projects, temporarily or indefinitely delay 44, and significantly modify 197 more."[10]

It should be understood, however, that the administrative reform accomplished through NEPA could not be instantaneous or wholly accomplished through mandatory procedures. The changes sought through NEPA were understood by its drafters to require time; a decade has been no more than time to learn how the act should be administered. Learning has occurred, and most of the criticisms leveled at the act in earlier years are no longer relevant.

The genius of NEPA lies in its linkage of mandatory procedure to substantive policy criteria and in the pressure it brings upon administrative agencies to consider scientific evidence in their planning and decisionmaking. NEPA is importantly, even though secondarily, a full disclosure or public participation law. Other statutes provide more explicitly for this procedural reform, although NEPA adds to their strength. More significant, perhaps, NEPA provides for a full display of environmental alternatives and consequences for review by responsible agency decisionmakers. The reality and significance of this innovative provision has been largely underplayed by commentators on NEPA.

In the course of a series of interviews in 1980 and 1981 with planning officials of the Bureau of Land Management, the Forest Service, and the Corps of Engineers, I asked whether NEPA principles would continue to be honored by the agencies should the act itself be repealed. Would the EIS process be continued in some form? In every case, the respondents, who were chiefly managers and engineers, not environmental scientists, believed that agency practice would continue substantially as it has been under the act. None considered that repeal or downgrading of NEPA would be desirable; they regarded its continuation as in the interest of the agencies as well as of the public. And they uniformly expressed the view that public expectations would not permit reversion to the practices of pre-NEPA days. Moreover, new employees, including engineers, were bringing into government the environmental values prevalent in their communities and to which they had been exposed during their formative years. Thus it may be that the reforms that NEPA has helped to institute may become the norms of the years ahead.

4
Impact Analysis:
An Instrument
of Policy

Before considering the uses of science in environmental impact analysis, it is necessary to identify the types of scientific methodology characteristically employed by government agencies in pursuit of their missions. The methods have been those developed in the specific sciences, for example in agronomy, forestry, microbiology, and hydrology. They have not only been directed in linear fashion toward specific points of inquiry but have often been characterized by reductionism, which is an effort to break down the components of a phenomenon into basic elements. Physics is the preeminent reductionist science. Although to say that reductionism seeks to understand phenomena by understanding the behavior of their most elementary parts and their relationship to one another is an oversimplification, this description does suggest a reductionist's approach to knowledge. A homely illustration would be an effort to understand the phenomenon of a clock by examining its individual parts and interworkings.

Historically, the characteristic applications of scientific method to public affairs and the private economy have resembled the approach of a reductionist scientist to understanding the phenomenon of the clock. Necessary as this approach is to understanding clocks as physical phenomena, it provides no information about how clocks are used, why they are used, and the consequences of their use. Clocks are components of the greater function of timekeeping in society, and understanding clocks as physical phenomena is not a bad analogy to understanding the components of environmental phenomena as a part of the physical sciences. The environmental problems of human society are both physical and social and for adequate understanding, require information from many sciences, but information integrated into intelligible propositions instead of a series of disjointed incremental reports regarding man's environmental interrelationships.

Disjointed incrementalism has, however, been a characteristic (but not invariably *the* characteristic) of public administration. Programs administered by federal agencies have been added incrementally by congressional action. For each statute of the Congress, standards and procedures may be specified, often in detail. To be responsive to the congressional mandate the agencies tend to segregate programs, especially if there is need to avoid comingling of funds. A result is a specialized use of science pursuant to specialized agency tasks. Categorical programs are not necessarily undesirable, but when numbers of them interrelate, as do the pollution control programs, the advantages of an integrated use of the sciences are apparent.

The attainment of an integrated interdisciplinary use of science is, of course, never more than imperfectly achieved. The merging of categorical pollution control programs in the EPA has never fully achieved the integration that was intended. But a fundamental part of the goal of the National Environmental Policy Act has been to move government science and administration from their traditional commitment to incremental specialization to an increasing emphasis upon an integrative syncretic approach to policymaking. It should be emphasized that this is not an "either/or" proposition; it is a "both" proposition. Syncretic science and administration are possible only when there is something to synthesize, and the synthesis is rarely better than its component parts.

Through Procedure to Policy

The power of modern science and technology to deliver what is asked of them and more makes "looking before leaping" a prudent axiom of policy. The perils of failing to take an adequate look before acting have now become so widely apparent that it seems improbable that government in the future will reduce the use of environmental impact analysis. On the contrary, a more extensive although certainly more focused and more meaningful use of impact assessment techniques seems probable.

NEPA is not the only legislation that has required looking before leaping. The same objective underlies the Technology Assessment Act of 1972. But the contrasting relationship of these acts to public administration is significant. The National Environmental Policy Act undertook fundamental policy reform primarily through procedure, and this reform was built into the structure and operations of the administrative agencies. The Technology Assessment Act, in contrast, established an office responsible to a committee of the Congress. Technology assessment occurred outside the administrative structure and, indeed, outside the executive branch of the federal government. Whereas the findings of technology assessments might have an impact upon agency planning and decisionmaking, it would be an impact from outside the agency. It would not necessarily "condition" the agency to make more prudent decisions in the future or equip the agency to better assess the multiple impacts of its proposed actions.

A president generally familiar with science and for whom environmental quality was a high priority concern could use his executive and constitutional responsibility to take care that the laws were faithfully executed, to persuade agencies to implement Section 102(2)(a) of NEPA, and to use a systematic interdisciplinary approach in planning and decisionmaking. In fact, it has been a very long time since a president of the United States has been familiar or perhaps even comfortable with science and scientists, and among recent presidents, only Jimmy Carter appears to have accorded environmental quality a high priority position in his administration. The threat of Russian technology rather than commitment to science or concern over environmental deterioration originally led to the creation of the Office of the Science Advisor to the President.

President Nixon found that his priorities did not justify the retention of this office. In principle, an observation that I made eight years ago is still true—failure of the National Environmental Policy Act to achieve its full potential has been to a large degree a consequence of presidential indifference or of insufficient understanding of the possibilities inherent in the act.[1] But responsibility for the shortfall in NEPA's potential must be shared at least equally by the Congress, which has too often enacted legislation as if NEPA had never existed.

In practice, this judgment must be qualified by President Carter's Executive Order 11991 of 24 May 1977, authorizing the Council on Environmental Quality to issue regulations having the force of law, and Executive Order 12114 of 4 January 1979, which clarified the application of NEPA to activities of federal agencies outside the geographical limits of United States jurisdiction. As of this writing, it would be premature to assess the Reagan response to NEPA. But nothing in Ronald Reagan's first year in the presidency suggests that his administration will do more than the minimum that the law requires in the implementation of NEPA. Whether it would seriously attempt to roll back environmental protection measures is conjectural; minimal enforcement appears to be a more probable prospect.

During the drafting of NEPA, consideration was given to requiring the Office of Management and Budget (OMB) or the General Accounting Office (GAO) to enforce agency compliance with the act, using fiscal controls as leverage. This line of implementation was not pursued, however, and it does not appear that any president has used the OMB effectively to obtain agency compliance with NEPA policy intent. Indeed, it is questionable whether the Office of Management and Budget has competence effectively to influence and coordinate agency policy with respect to primarily scientific and noneconomic considerations. The General Accounting Office has on occasion reviewed and commented upon agency compliance with NEPA. But the GAO reports have been more in the nature of obiter dicta than prescriptive orders, and no agency expenditure has ever been disallowed for failure to comply with NEPA. It has remained for the courts to suspend a sword of Damocles, in the form of an injunction, over the agencies. Thus, whatever the predilections of agency administrators, and they are not necessarily adverse to NEPA objectives, the prospect of judicial review has been sufficient to influence agency use of science in the service of policy to the extent necessary to satisfy the courts that "the agency reached its decision after a full, good faith consideration and balancing of environmental factors."[2]

Section 102(2)(a) of NEPA, for example, requires federal agencies to follow a systematic, interdisciplinary approach to ensure the integrated use of the natural and social sciences and environmental design arts in planning and decisionmaking. This provision by itself might be difficult to enforce, but the EIS requirement, amended by the regulations, gives it teeth. How much bite the teeth have is questionable; noncompliance might be difficult to prove. Coercion ought not to be necessary to force action that our present state of knowledge tells us is the sensible and safe way to examine decisions that may have significant environmental and social consequences. Some agencies do not need to be pressured to comply because the interdisciplinary mandate of NEPA is being routinely and effectively observed.

The Systematic Interdisciplinary Approach

Both the terms *interdisciplinary* and *systematic* are subject to interpretation. Absent the EIS requirement, agencies would not find it difficult to satisfy the courts that both prescriptions had been observed in their planning and decisionmaking. In answering to the five points upon which statements must be made under Section 102(2)(c), however, agencies can hardly avoid disclosing the extent to which they have in fact drawn upon the sciences that are relevant to the environmental issue at hand. Moreover, under the regulations issued by the CEQ under the authority granted by Executive Order 11991, the agency is required to identify in its impact statement the scientific experts who contributed to its drafting.

The CEQ regulations requiring scoping also push the agency toward interdisciplinary involvement. Scoping is a process by which the environmental implications of a proposed action are examined from a variety of disciplinary perspectives to ascertain its substantive scope. All of the agencies that might in some way be concerned with the impact of a proposed action are represented in examining the broad ramifications of the proposed action, and in this act of identification a broad array of sciences may need to be invoked. In any event, it is plausible (but perhaps unrealistic) to suppose that even a nonscientist acting in the capacity of a federal judge could identify the principal sciences that should have had an input into the scoping exercise.

William H. Rodgers correctly observes that the purpose of the systematic interdisciplinary requirement is "to assure that the environmental effects of a project are understood fully, and addressed on the merits." Thus Section 102(2)(a) supports the opinions of the courts that an agency

> must disclose and consider responsible opposing scientific opinions, coordinate expertise within the agency, expand its staff to accommodate environmental evaluations, respond to concerns raised by experts it retains, sponsor research on important issues either as a pre-condition or concurrently with implementation of a project, answer or perhaps even defer to expert criticism or recommendations from other agencies, actively seek out (as distinguished from passively absorbing) expert advice and opposing opinions, or engage in actual consultation with other agencies.[3]

The extent to which the NEPA requirement of a "systematic" approach has been reflected in agency performance is difficult to ascertain. Systematic planning certainly was practiced in many federal agencies before enactment of NEPA, perhaps the most notable example being the space exploration efforts undertaken through the National Aeronautics and Space Administration that culminated in the Apollo XI landing upon the moon. The term "systematic" is itself ambiguous, answering to a number of different meanings.

The term was probably preferable to "systems" approach because by the late 1960s the word "systems" as used in planning had acquired a very special meaning growing out of World War II operations research and suggesting to many people an abstract, quantified investigation. The term "systematic" as used in NEPA was much less precise and was intended to indicate that the dimensions of planning corresponded to the dimensions of the problem it directed. In other words, planning should take into account the complexity and the scope of the total system upon which the planning would have an impact.

As with the term "interdisciplinary," "systematic" in NEPA should not be understood as standing alone, for Section 102(2)is a coherent phrase that also specifies the integrated (not fragmentary) use of the natural sciences. Agencies could show a long history of systematic multidisciplinary planning that would still fall far short of considering important elements in the total system under investigation or even considering the total system, even when feasible. The 1944 Pick-Sloan compromise plan for developing the Missouri River basin, named for the respective heads of the Corps of Engineers and the Bureau of Reclamation, is a notable case in point. To resolve a quarrel over who was to develop the Missouri River and head off a threatened Missouri Valley Authority, like TVA, the two agencies divided responsibility for the river basin. The corps took the lower half for navigation and flood control; the bureau took the upper half for hydropower and irrigation.[4]

During the 1960s the use of the ecosystem concept in land use and resources planning and the application of systems concepts to the analysis of urban and regional development provided new methods for implementing a systematic, interdisciplinary, integrated approach to decisionmaking. Section 102(2)(h) of NEPA, requiring agencies to "initiate and utilize ecological information in the planning and development of resource-oriented projects," reinforced whatever inclinations agency planners may have had toward systematic interdisciplinary planning.

The NEPA mandate and paralleling statutes such as the Federal Land Policy and Management Act of 1976 (FLPMA) have necessitated large-scale, complex, interdisciplinary environmental planning studies. The federal agencies have had to learn how to organize and manage such studies; before 1970 few had attempted comprehensive interdisciplinary planning, especially in areas of intense public controversy. Planning for large engineering projects, such as the Panama Canal or the Apollo program, was essentially to implement policy already made and uncomplicated by cross-currents of local politics. But impact analysis and planning under the environmental statutes of the 1970s were required as input to policy and decision-making. Although general policies might be adopted prior to environmental impact analysis and planning, major findings regarding effects of land use, resource development, and public access, among others, could substantially alter the details of policy, affecting the conflicting preferences of politically active citizens.

An example of the difficulties inherent in large-scale interdisciplinary environmental planning under political pressure was the Bureau of Land Management's California Desert Plan.[5] Preparation of this plan was required by FLPMA, which closely paralleled NEPA in its procedural requirements; its story deserves (and would require) a case study exceeding the space available here. But certain lessons can be derived from even a cursory examination of what happened. Impact analysis was undertaken by a large resource team (at least fifty professionals plus contract personnel). This group was separated from the planning group and the entire enterprise separated from the local BLM management. Coordination of this diverse group of specialists was never given the attention that the integrative aspect of the task required. Some of the science professionals had motives inconsistent with planning goals which, in many cases, appear to have been unclear to them. Some saw opportunity to advance their own research or science careers; others found occasion to confront BLM management policies from within. Other obstacles to effective planning included the fractionalized pattern of land ownership and statutory deadlines for completion. But the primary cause of difficulty in the history of the California Desert Plan was failure to understand that the requirement of an integrated interdisciplinary approach to planning required appropriate innovations in administrative organization and procedure.

Two factors in particular complicate the achievement of comprehensive integrated interdisciplinary planning. The first of these is the practical task of coordinating the work of diverse disciplinary specialists toward a coherent assessment of the environmental implications of action alternatives. Disparate scientific findings alone do not provide an adequate basis for planning and decisionmaking. This point is obvious; but how the coordinative, integrative objective is to be accomplished within the usual constraints of time, money, and legal provisions is much less apparent. A second complicating factor is prior commitment—the necessity to accommodate incompatible political priorities. Government has customarily undertaken commitments and made decisions without regard to all of the consequences or side effects of their implementation. When political commitments precede comprehensive environmental analysis, it is unrealistic to expect that an agency's environmental impact assessment will be pushed to the point that the agency officials will feel compelled to retract earlier commitments. Nevertheless, the science requirements of NEPA, even when brushed aside, remain as a kind of Banquo's ghost at the banquet table—environmental lawsuits threatening the smooth development of agency plans.

Political considerations are always present in public planning and decisionmaking. Public policies inevitably confront an existing reality, involving commitments that must somehow be accommodated. A factor critical to this accommodation is the character of project or program planning in which significant environmental impacts are implicit and public conflict is present. The management task is to assist the development of a collective competence among disciplinary specialists to develop the data needed for policy-relevant planning and decisionmaking. This task does not imply a distorting of objective science to avoid embarrassment to public officials or the selective omission of relevant evidence from impact statements or planning documents. Accommodation need not mean capitulation. What is required is an interactive process among science analysts and program planners that will draw from scientific investigations the range and details of evidence that will enable policymakers to arrive at decisions consistent with the mandates of the laws. In the California Desert Plan the various pieces of scientific evidence often failed to mesh, the resource specialists and planners held to differing criteria of relevance, and results of fieldwork sometimes arrived too late to meet mandatory planning deadlines.

Under the circumstances of writing the EIS for the California Desert Plan it is not surprising that not all participants shared the same perceptions of the task. Officials in the Forest Service and the Corps of Engineers, as well as in the BLM, have frequently observed that scientists and technicians newly arrived in an agency or employed in impact assessment find it difficult to adapt their expertise to the NEPA process. Previous training has often inculcated self-reliance and exhaustive coverage of detail as professional virtues. To be asked to focus on specific impacts rather than upon the entire phenomenon under study, and perhaps to make concessions to variant viewpoints of other disciplines, may strike a new staff member as unprofessional. Most science professionals joining an interdisciplinary environmental assessment team adapt to the task. True interdisciplinary integration sometimes occurs, especially when a group of five or six individuals work together over a period of months under an effective team leader.

Having met with interdisciplinary teams in three major federal agencies in different locations and at different times, I am satisfied that the interdisciplinary integrated approach to agency planning does occur and is effective. I would not assume that interdisciplinary teamwork always occurs where it should, or that it is always effective. But senior employees in the Corps of Engineers, the Forest Service, and the BLM have said that it seldom occurred before NEPA.

The Forest Service has taken seriously the commitment to interdisciplinary planning. Christopher K. Leman observes that "the emphasis is on interdisciplinary planning; even the multidisciplinary approach of the 1970s, the Forest Service now confesses, was insufficiently integrated."[6] Regulations in 1978 implementing the National Forest Management Act of 1976 in the spirit of NEPA required each National Forest to establish an interdisciplinary planning team.

An illustrative case of interdisciplinarity in planning and impact analysis has been the response of the Forest Service to a proposal from the Lomex Corporation to prospect for uranium in the Los Padres National Forest of California. Under the leadership of District Ranger Keith Guenther and Environmental Impact Forester Christine Rose, a team of experts from within the Forest Service and from associated agencies developed a draft impact statement addressing such diverse issues as water quality, surface radiation, area geology, cultural resources, and threatened or endangered plant and animal species. Participating on the team were external representatives from San Luis Obispo County, the California Regional Water Quality Board, the Environmental Protection Agency, the Native American Heritage Commission, the U.S. Geological Survey, and the Bureau of Mines. A much larger number of state and federal agencies were involved on a consulting basis. Whatever may be said of the Forest Service's decision on the Lomex proposal, it did not act without full disclosure of all relevant circumstances. And having observed the team in action and talked individually with several of its members, I believe that the approach being taken is as interdisciplinary as anyone could reasonably expect. It wholly epitomizes the interdisciplinary precept of NEPA.

The Bureau of Reclamation's environmental impact analysis for the Garrison Diversion Project illustrates the difficulty of reconciling systematic interdisciplinary planning that addresses the full dimensions of a project with the political commitments and importunities that push the agency in directions that NEPA would indicate it ought not to go. For an environmental impact statement to be adequate, a full range of relevant sciences needs to be invoked. The agency is placed in a position of risking defeat in the courts if it fails to consider the full dimensions of the environmental problems or of risking administrative disallowance if project modification as a result of the environmental impact analysis throws the project into an unacceptable cost-benefit ratio. The Bureau of Reclamation found itself in this situation in analyzing the environmental impacts of the Garrison Diversion Project. Failing fully to assess the possible environmental consequences of the project in Canada, the bureau developed a cost-benefit ratio that depended upon the completion of those parts of the project that, as it turned out, would have environmental impacts in Canada to which the Canadian government objected. Should the project as fully planned be found in contravention of the Boundary Waters Treaty of 1909 and should the United States government desist from developing those parts affecting Canada, full completion of the remainder of the project would be based on political fiat in nonconformity with the economic justification originally required by Congress for the project, as for other comparable water projects.[7]

Of course, agencies have selectively used systematic and limited interdisciplinary planning to develop cost-benefit ratios. But when environmental impact analysis has employed systematic and interdisciplinary methodology, relatively unbiased by agency preference, the agency's environmental analysis has sometimes substantially refuted its cost-benefit allegations. This occurred in the case of the proposed Big Pine Reservoir in Indiana, where the Corps of Engineers' environmental impact statement provided evidence that could be read to indicate that the project would be economically as well as ecologically unsound. The corps consequently withdrew the project; a decade earlier it probably would have been constructed because its negative effects probably would not have been thoroughly investigated.

It should be clear that the EIS does not determine policy but that it does raise presumptions that administrative decisionmakers must taken into account. The disclosure in the draft statement of the possible environmental impacts of a proposed action and statements regarding the alternatives considered and the balance of long-term and short-term effects place the agency in a potentially vulnerable position if its case is not soundly based. The practical test of the political effectiveness of an EIS is the extent to which agency plans are revised or rescinded as a result of environmental impact analysis. If one assumes that the federal agencies generally analyze the consequences of possible courses of action at preproposal stages and have no intention to degrade the environment, deliberately and unnecessarily, it should be expected that the majority of proposals would remain intact with analysis. But one would also expect that given the history of single-track planning and politically inspired projects, some percentage of them might be severely modified or fall by the wayside. In fact, this is what the evidence appears to show.[8]

The most recent studies on the implementation of NEPA have concluded that multidisciplinary science is generally being integrated into the planning processes of the major resource management agencies. This development results directly from procedural requirements in NEPA for science, notably Sections 102(2) (a), (b), (c), and (h), and indirectly from agency action needed to implement these provisions. The most obvious action has been to employ more science specialists. Specialties only occasionally required may be obtained through consultation. But for the big resource agencies the needs of daily business, complicated by the growth of policy-relevant scientific knowledge (for example, in geology and biology), have resulted in greatly increased numbers and specialties among scientific personnel.

These scientific and environmental professionals have developed informal networks for communication within and even between agencies. Wildlife biologists in the Fish and Wildlife Service often know counterparts in the National Park Service, and geologists in the Forest Service have contacts in the Geological Survey. But unlike the bounded environment of disciplines in academia, the increasingly multidimensional character of public programs requires interaction among the science disciplines involved—limnologists with hydrologists, geologists with botanists, chemists with agronomists. The systematic interdisciplinary approach requirement of NEPA has, in effect, reinforced a trend already under way when the environmental movement gained momentum. But NEPA and its implementing regulations have broadened and systematized this trend, providing greater assurance that the systematic interdisciplinary approach would occur when and where needed.

Even without NEPA, numerous federal statutes and executive orders require both multidisciplinary and interdisciplinary approaches. A variety of collateral statutes may apply to any given agency action (e.g., civil rights, labor standards, occupational safety). An agency proposing action that entails environmental impacts will have to develop a prospective list of statutory measures of which account must be taken. For some proposals the statutes to be observed could be numerous. Any of the following examples from a longer possible list might need to be considered:

> Antiquities Act of 1906
> Fish and Wildlife Coordination Act of 1934
> Historic Sites Act of 1935
> Wilderness Act of 1964
> National Historic Preservation Act of 1966
> National Wild and Scenic Rivers Act of 1968
> National Trails System Act of 1968
> Endangered Species Conservation Act of 1969
> Federal Water Pollution Control Act of 1972
> Clean Air Act Amendments of 1977
> American Indian Religious Freedom Resolution of 1978

The basic organic statutes of some agencies contain major environmental policy requirements that reinforce or extend NEPA provisions. Among these are the Federal Land Policy and Management Act of 1976 and the National Forest Management Act of 1976. The Surface Mining Control and Reclamation Act of 1977 presents another set of environmental issues to be considered in situations where it applies.

The NEPA process provides a modus operandi whereby all relevant statutory requirements, executive orders, and regulations may be taken into account in a systematic and integrated manner. The process is complex; it consumes time and requires money. So also does managing a modern hospital, operating a global telecommunications system, or exploring the moon. No less than in these examples, failure to take account of all factors significant to the outcome of an environmental impacting action could result in unintended consequences. To ascertain the true scope of the environmental consequences of a proposed flood-control dam is no less reasonable than to be aware of the scope of effects that could follow a surgical operation, and more lives might be affected in the former case.

As previously noted, the scoping process required under the CEQ regulations brings together, in the early stages of a proposed action, representatives of all agencies presumed to be affected. Thus the probability is increased that the full range of relevant factors will be considered and a mismatching or conflict of agency plans can be identified in the very early stages. Moreover, the requirement under Section 102(2) (c) that impact statements be circulated among all agencies affected, not only federal but also state and local, enables coordinative action to be taken. At the least it can help prevent conflicting action being taken inadvertently and provides additional opportunity for disciplinary inputs that might have been missed in scoping.

NEPA scholars and the courts have given insufficient attention to the requirement of an "integrated use of the natural and social sciences and environmental design arts." In chapter 5, I will return at length to the integrative function of NEPA. It is sufficient here to observe that it is even more difficult to ascertain that integrative use has been made of science in planning and decisionmaking than that systematic interdisciplinary approaches have been taken. But integrated use is an explicitly stated purpose of the systematic and interdisciplinary approach. Without this integrated use of the natural and social sciences and environmental design arts, systematic and interdisciplinary approaches could be no better than the compromises incorporated into many interagency comprehensive plans, which were largely composites of the special mission projects of the participating agencies.

Institutionalizing Policy through People

In addition to their role in implementing the interdisciplinary requirements of NEPA, people are indispensable in institutionalizing its goals and procedures throughout the federal service. This process of institutionalization can be conceptualized conveniently by noting the relationships among purposes, procedures, positions, and people.

The goals of NEPA declared in Section 101 are specific enough for policy purposes and are vague only to those who apparently regard the act primarily as regulatory. Persons familiar with recent advancements in the natural and social sciences would find more meaning in the declaration of goals in Title I than would persons unfamiliar with the concepts behind the words. For example, behind such objectives as preserving "an environment which supports diversity, and variety of individual choice" (Section 101(b)(4)) and balancing "population and resource use" (Section 101(b)(5)), there is a scientific literature familiar to many environmental specialists if not to most lawyers and the general public and their political representatives.

The policy effectiveness of NEPA is, as we know, to be found in its mandatory procedures, especially those specified in Section 102(2)(c) and the implementing regulations of the CEQ and the respective agencies. But to implement these procedures, people are needed, and positions must be established to provide the structure through which procedures are carried out. These positions are essential to the ability of their incumbents to advance the purposes of NEPA within the agencies. And they symbolize in a very concrete way the fact that the National Environmental Policy Act is an integral part of the legislative mandate of each federal agency.

Executive Order 11991 of 24 May 1977, giving the regulations of the CEQ the force of law, is important in providing a legal foundation supportive of the efforts of environmental science specialists within the agencies, first, to legitimize and to maintain their control over evidence and data regarding the environmental impact of agency proposals, and, second, to strengthen their leverage upon the agency not only to observe honesty and scientific integrity in impact statements but to use scientific concepts and methods in agency planning and decisionmaking in a manner consistent with the NEPA mandate.

An intangible but creative aspect of this institutionalization process might be called interdisciplinary learning. Mutual exchanges of information and viewpoints occur through the interaction of specialists from the various sciences with agency personnel in task forces and project planning committees. Given the traditionally narrow focus of professional education in such fields as agriculture, forestry, engineering, and law, it seems probable that many agency administrators and technicians could benefit from information and ideas that were not a part of their academic or agency experiences.

It has been estimated that in the beginning of the 1980s as many as three thousand environmental "specialists" were employed throughout the federal service because of NEPA. Not all of these, to be sure, were capable of contributing significantly to intra-agency education but, both formally and informally, many have. Collectively, although not always individually, they are a leavening influence, heightening an awareness throughout the federal service that more than specific mission goals must be considered in defining the objectives of public action. And considering the strategic if relatively low-level position that environmental specialists occupy in many of the agencies and the procedural requirements that support the legitimacy of their analyses and advice, it seems reasonable to suppose that their presence could be significant in building awareness and perhaps even observance of the goals and values enumerated in Title I of NEPA into the normal expectations of agency administration.[9]

In addressing a symposium of the American Meteorological Society in 1976, Lewis M. Branscomb, former director of the

National Bureau of Standards and at the time chief scientist and vice-president of IBM, declared his belief that the invention of the concept and mechanism of environmental impact assessments, embodied in the National Environmental Policy Act, was "one of the most significant institutional developments of recent history." Later in the symposium discussion, he spoke of the need for a new kind of research to back up environmental impact analysis—"an institutional invention required for an Environmental Impact Statement." He said that "institutions are the way in which we embody a process in some structure with some habits and identifiable responsibilities of the individual to conduct the process." He proposed establishment of a group of not-for-profit institutions financed in part through public appropriations and in part through endowment to address the full spectrum of issues to be balanced, "not as a substitute for the political process but relevant to its needs."[10]

In my view, Branscomb's proposal is even more pertinent today than it was in 1976 because our perception of need for knowledge to cope with our problems has deepened. We do not have institutional arrangements sufficient to undertake timely and comprehensive investigation of unresolved questions. The institutionalization of NEPA through a new type of environmental science professional has been a necessary but insufficient step toward the goals that NEPA declares for the nation. In chapter 5, I will examine some possible reasons for the lack of positive response to Branscomb's proposal and to others like it and indicate how, by an ad hoc process, some of his ideas of institutionalization through people are being realized.

Impact Analysis as Policy Strategy

Marshall McLuhan's aphorism that "the medium is the message" might be extended to broad areas of public administration as "the procedure is the policy." The history of environmental policy, as federal courts have declared, "may well prove to be the history of observance of procedural safeguards."[11] This statement makes sense when it is recognized that to implement a policy there must be appropriate procedures and that the procedures ultimately have an impact upon the execution of the policy. The National Environmental Policy Act presents one of the more clearly defined examples of this point. But distinction must be drawn between the NEPA 102(2)(c) process and the larger body of departmental planning and decisionmaking with which the NEPA process is presumably integrated.

Whatever else it is, the EIS requirement of NEPA is a policy strategy. It was proposed in my testimony on 16 April 1969 before the Senate Committee on Interior and Insular Affairs explicitly as an "action-forcing" mechanism. Its other purposes—to provide for judicial review and to facilitate public disclosure—were recognized but considered secondary to the action-forcing purpose. If the environmental impact statement requirement had not been invented, it seems highly probable that some comparable means of impact assessment would have found its way into the law of federal procedures. In fact, other mechanisms have been developed and applied.

Technology assessment, for example, is not only the function of a special office created by Congress but is undertaken in several different federal agencies. Conventional cost-benefit analysis has become more inclusive and sophisticated and, as "extended" cost-benefit analysis, properly includes many of the considerations that are implicit in environmental impact assessment. Indeed, some policy researchers tend to regard the environmental impact statement, technology assessment, extended cost-benefit analysis, and social accounting as particular aspects of a more comprehensive impact analysis. It would not be surprising, a century hence, if there are still government programs to analyze, there will be one comprehensive science of policy impact analysis and the present categories and perhaps others yet unidentified will be regarded as interrelating subsets of a more comprehensive whole.

Although an EIS of itself establishes no policy or rule, the procedures by which an EIS is prepared under regulations promulgated by the CEQ have been found by Judge J. Skelly Wright of the United States Court of Appeals for the District of

Columbia Circuit to be subject to requirements "not significantly different" from those applied by the courts under Section
553 (Title V, U.S. Code) of the federal Administrative Procedure Act. "No principled distinction," Judge Wright declared,
"can be made between EIS preparation and informal rulemaking with respect to the need of both to comply with Section 553
of the APA." Thus "those who have responsibility for environmental impact statements should make certain that their
preparation and execution comply meticulously with the requirements not only of NEPA, but also the informal rulemaking procedures of the APA as most recently and rigorously
interpreted by the courts."[12]

This stricture reinforces what has already been said regarding the use of a procedure—the EIS—as an instrument of a
policy. To the extent that policy implementation depends upon
the procedures, the more strictly it must be observed and the
more important is its effectiveness in obtaining compliance
with the policy. The CEQ regulations, supplemented by the
agencies, link together the several subsections of NEPA Section 102 so that procedure and policy are as opposite sides of the
same coin.

It is commonplace that results of analytic methods carefully
applied and professing scientific objectivity are not necessarily
welcomed by politicians and mission-oriented administrators.
Moreover, it may be argued that science is itself a bias and that
on many issues scientists have been substantively prejudiced
beyond the data that tested evidence confirms. Nevertheless,
the legal right of access to public information and, in general,
the open character of science, increase the probability that
scientific error either inadvertent or intentional will be exposed and corrected. But administrative or political error
might likewise be exposed, at cost to the ambitions and dignity
of public officials.

As science uncovers previously unperceived linkages and
effects in man's impacts upon the environment, the legal requirement that serious account be taken of this evidence places
constraints on politically inspired policy. More accurately, it
changes the context and ground rules of political action. Al-

though it cannot be assumed that political fiat will refrain from efforts to override impolitic evidence, as in the 1953 battery additive controversy involving the firing of the director of the National Bureau of Standards or in the burning of the 1957 population estimates in the U.S. Department of Agriculture, scientific methodology and public information are narrowing the margin of freedom to impose arbitrary political decisions.

Advances in scientific knowledge and methodology regarding environmental consequences of human activities have changed the conditions of risk with which public decisionmakers must live. Scientific knowledge has become applicable in ways that have greatly increased the risks incurred in its use, for example, in nuclear technology, genetic engineering, and chemical psychotherapy. Developing also, but less rapidly, have been techniques of impact analysis and, more broadly, of policy analysis. Thus although human welfare may be more than ever at stake in public decisions, there is also less excuse than ever for blundering into disaster in these decisions.

Impact analysis offers a means toward risk reduction that administrators generally are unlikely voluntarily to relinquish. In the private sector as well as in government, decisionmakers can scarcely avoid noticing the tendency of the judiciary to find that humans are legally entitled to be protected against man-made environmental hazards. Courts award punishing damages against government agencies and officials who are responsible for the infliction of avoidable environmental damage upon humans. It therefore follows that impact analysis becomes an instrument of policy to protect agencies as well as the public. One is reminded that the inspection and grading of meat for public protection, once resisted by the meat-packing industry, has become a widely advertised symbol of product reliability and now protects the interests of the company as much as the consumer.

Impact analysis has generated a cycle of policy development that has self-maintaining tendencies. Examination of the possible environmental consequences of proposed action has three systemic effects. First, in each agency in which environmental impacts are significant, it necessitates a cadre of scientific and technical specialists whose skills must be concerted toward integrated findings and whose focus is on the effects of the agency mission instead of exclusively on mission objectives. In effect, a permanent course-correcting mechanism has been built into the "normal" bureaucracy. Second, the findings resulting from impact analysis may not only alter existing proposals but may influence future considerations of agency policy. Third, the areas of scientific and technological inadequacy that impact analysis may reveal feed back into the perceptions that scientists and engineers have of their disciplines and of the need and priorities of future research. This third phase of the cycle is the subject of the following chapter.

5
Feedback Effects:
Policy Influences Science

NEPA has been influential in at least three directions: (1) toward public policy and administration, (2) toward public participation in policymaking, and (3) toward science in all four senses of the term as used here—method, substance, occupation, and application. These several impacts of NEPA cannot be precisely delineated because NEPA is an expression of a larger movement toward the protection and improvement of the environment. NEPA is an exceptional act of legislation, but it is not the only statute dealing with environmental affairs or having impacts on science and society. It should not, therefore, be inferred that there is an exclusive one-to-one relationship between NEPA and developments in the field now generally termed "environmental science." There have, however, been reciprocal influences between policy and science, and NEPA has had a strong and positive influence upon the development of environmental research and education.

This influence has been incremental and directional rather than universal or absolute. The emergence of an aggregative environmental science in no way diminishes and is indeed dependent upon the many specific sciences that have contributed to a larger understanding of the total environment. The influence of NEPA and associated environmental legislation should be understood as "transforming," in an additive sense.

A rough analogy may be drawn between environmental science and its components and between biology and its constituent sciences. There is a difference, however, inasmuch as the

relationships between environmental science and its components are more diverse and less easily defined than those
relating to biology. Skeptics can be found who doubt that environmental science exists other than in name. Yet if we look at
the history of science and the growth of knowledge and of
scholarly disciplines, it appears that there is nothing unique or
even unusual about the emergence of the environment as a
focus for an integrative and aggregative science.

In summary, we can identify at least four respects in which
NEPA and its associated environmental statutes have had an
impact upon the development of science. Key words identifying
the feedback effect of NEPA upon science are (1) applicative, (2)
aggregative, (3) synthesizing, and (4) professionalizing.

From Theory toward Practice

Before NEPA, in the middle 1960s and notably during the
89th Congress, environmental protection legislation was being
proposed which depended for its advocacy upon science-derived
information. Legislation to combat air and water pollution, to
assess the effects of pesticides, and to encourage improved
disposal of solid wastes, in particular, needed to be science-
based. If environmental regulations were not to be found arbitrary and capricious by the courts, some reasonable relationship must be made evident between the rules governing
discharge of contaminants into the environment and their
resulting damage to health, safety, or economic welfare.

From the outset of the environmental movement, the adequacy of science to support environmental standards and regulations has been a continuing point of controversy. Only in the
relatively recent past have courts accepted the concept that
synergistic effects such as photochemical smog justify public
regulation of private behavior. It was often impossible to prove
that any particular ingredient emitted into the atmosphere
had a demonstrable and specific effect upon the health of a
particular individual. And even today biomedical evidence
linking the incidence of black lung and brown lung disease to

cigarette smoking does not appear to have obtained political or judicial acceptance.

As the environmental movement gained momentum and as demand for environmental protective legislation increased, the inadequacy of science to provide firm support for policy objectives became increasingly apparent. Promoters of science in environmental legislation were frequently disappointed to discover its lack for direct applicability to problems of planning and decisionmaking. The keystone science of the environment was ecology, which was regarded during the 1960s as being relatively undeveloped and sometimes as lacking the requisite attributes of a "science." But when the state of the environment became a public issue, there was clearly evident need for developing a vehicle for the integrative application of interdisciplinary scientific knowledge to environmental problems.

Although this need was not answered by the more precise meaning of ecology preferred by some scientists, ecology, in the popular perception, became *the* environmental science. The news media contributed to a very broad, colloquial usage, so that for many people ecology and environmental science became synonymous. Yet behind this perceptual confusion there was awareness of the need for a more coherent, integrative use of science in the analysis and solution of environmental problems. A higher level of integration was required in the hierarchy of knowledge—a coordinative discipline of environmental relationships. Ecology, in its precise sense, was not the appropriate name for this "umbrella" discipline, if at this stage it could be called a discipline.

The term that has seemed to gain acceptance has been "environmental science," as evidenced by the frequency of its appearance in academic curricula and degrees. By 1981, environmental impact assessment in at least several major federal agencies was achieving a procedural integration of relevant sciences, a practice not evident in the earlier history of the NEPA process. But science professionals were learning to integrate their expertise with that of others on the job. Many of them declared that they were becoming "interdisciplinary" in the sense that mutual learning was occurring among the members of interdisciplinary teams. But could they have been better prepared for the tasks of interdisciplinary analysis during previous academic training? Many agency managers and staff members have thought so.

NEPA, and the environmental movement generally, not only forced ecology in its more precise sense to reconsider its status, but required its extension from a science that was largely theoretical and descriptive to one that was integrative and practical. Theoretical ecology was of little practical value to administrative decisionmakers who needed an applied ecology that would answer the "what if?" problems of environmental decisionmaking.

During the early years of the environmental movement, there was much frustration among legislators and public administrators charged with responsibility for environment-affecting decisions. The complaint was often heard among public officials that they could not get straightforward, unequivocal, relevant answers from scientists. They could get little help in estimating the risks that their decisions might entail.

Adding to the public administrators' frustration with ecologists was the practical necessity to employ more of them in meeting the requirements of the National Environmental Policy Act. NEPA was described by some cynics as the "catalytic converter" that made all kinds of people into "instant ecologists." It is certain that the requirements of Section 102(2)(c) in NEPA caused federal agencies to add to their staffs persons with training in ecology, but not many of these had been accustomed to the actual application of ecological principles to a wide range of environmental problems involving many more sciences and disciplines than ecology. The EIS requirement created an immediate practical necessity for a reorientation of science that was being felt in relation to science generally—a need to apply scientific information and method to problems of social concern.

Throughout the history of science in America, opinion regarding the relevance of research to society has varied in response to social circumstances.[1] Neither the public nor its officials have drawn sharp distinctions between science and technology. Pure or basic science, detached from social issues, has found advocacy primarily among physical scientists. But arguments for the public support of science have more often emphasized practical benefits. In time of war, science has been mobilized in the public service. Yet the application of science (or technology) to peacetime concerns has been a continuing theme among some advocates of public support for science.

During the Progressive Era, characterizing much of the first quarter of the nineteenth century, social purpose was a widely accepted rationale for science. But following World War I the focus of concern tended to shift toward private and industrial applications. During the depression years, government support for science, notably through the U.S. Department of Agriculture, emphasized practical applications—largely technological. During and after World War II, weapons systems and defense-related research became the rationale for federal support of science.

This rationale served the interests of many physical and biomedical scientists who found ways to carry on basic research in pursuit of practical application. But large areas of biology and social science generally found little support in defense-related arguments. Moreover, some physical scientists, and especially the younger ones, grew increasingly unhappy with the commitment of science to nuclear and biochemical weaponry and to the application of science-based technology to the war in Southeast Asia (for example, use of defoliants such as Agent Orange).

The popular ecology movement therefore opened an opportunity for a renewed commitment of science to peacetime purposes. Scientists were prominent in the environmental action groups that took form in the early 1960s. The Congress felt the pressure of public discontent with a perceived failure of government to bring science to bear upon the everyday problems of polluted air and water and hazardous materials. The result of these developments, noted in Chapter 2, was a partial but significant reorientation of focus among the sciences and in the allocation of public financial and institutional support. And this new commitment, viewed with misgiving by some science conservatives, became in itself a force, generating feedback into science in the universities and professional associations of scientists.

In 1971 President Richard Nixon proposed (but ultimately did not support) a federally assisted environmental policy research institute, and the Ecological Society of America established a section on applied ecology. Also in the early 1970s members of the Ecological Society of America, assisted by a grant from the National Science Foundation, began to develop The Institute of Ecology (TIE), a multidisciplinary, multi-institutional arrangement, international in sponsorship, and not only directed toward scientific investigations in ecology but also providing for a division concerned with environmental policy and an assembly that represented the interested and concerned public. Not all ecologists felt comfortable with the idea of a division for policy studies and a public assembly attached to a "scientific" institution. Nevertheless, it is significant that the ecologist members of the planning committee (which included some of the most highly qualified and widely respected scientists in the profession) regarded applied ecology as an instrument of public policy.

During the 1960s, a number of universities, assisted by the National Science Foundation, established programs of research and teaching in science and public policy. At least several of these programs emphasized environmental consequences of technoscientific innovation. Concern with science policy and its implications for society was reflected in several new journals. One of the earliest was the *Bulletin of the Atomic Scientists,* founded in 1945 in response to anxiety over nuclear weaponry and its consequences. Two decades later the focus of concern had shifted to more generalized impacts of science on society and the environment.

Initiation of the journal *Technological Forecasting and Social Change* in 1969 reflected this concern. As early as 1963 some scientists, including ecologists, established the Scientists Institute for Public Information (SIPI) for the purpose of bringing to public attention scientific findings regarding hazards of science-based technology, initially focusing on the issue of nuclear fallout. In 1973 SIPI adopted as its official journal the magazine *Environment,* which, beginning in 1958, had been published as *Scientist and Citizen* by the Greater St. Louis Citizens Committee for Nuclear Information. Reflecting the changing times, the journal's name was changed with its eleventh volume in 1969.

Thus the advent of environmental science occurred as an aspect of a more general public concern over the impacts of science and technology on society. The resulting requirements of environmental legislation in general, and of NEPA in particular, created a need for applied ecology, which in turn not only stimulated a professional concern among ecologists to see that the need was properly met but also created institutional arrangements for the application of ecological knowledge and principles to problems of policy. In 1974, under contract to the Corps of Engineers, The Institute of Ecology published a nine-volume *Directory of Environmental Life Scientists.* The rationale for government support for this compilation was the evident and urgent need of the agencies to identify persons capable of undertaking the environmental impact analyses that NEPA required.

NEPA clearly stimulated new emphases in the sciences. Gary W. Barrett of the Miami University Institute of Environmental Sciences and Department of Zoology and the National Science Foundation comments:

> Partially as a result of NEPA, new fields of study, such as ecosystem analysis, resource science, systems theory, stress ecology and environmental science, gained stature as vital new areas of study—areas which tended to merge the basic (liberal arts) and the applied (mission-oriented) schools of knowledge. Further, environmental manpower trends based on a traditional disciplinary input became somewhat antiquated, academic curricula required a new educational philosophy, and various organizations became involved in "retooling" personnel in "futuristic" impact assessment techniques and methodologies.[2]

Aggregative and Integrative Science

In the advancement of knowledge, the practical necessity to focus upon manageable research problems has been the con-

ventional explanation for a specialized science. The in-depth
pursuit of knowledge, commonly called reductionism, has been
highly successful in revealing how things work in particular
but has been less successful in showing how things work in
general. To understand the principles explaining the broadening gradations of generality encountered in environmental
problem solving, an increasing number of organized bodies of
knowledge or disciplines is required. To understand the behavior of large geophysical, ecological, and social systems, the
amount of information required can be so large and its elements so diverse as to defy comprehension. Merely to aggregate
knowledge from the sciences does not provide a coherent picture of a functioning system; appropriate structuring of knowledge is essential to interdisciplinary integration. As previously
noted, one may catalog and describe the parts of a clock or the
organs and processes of the human body and yet be far from
understanding how clocks or humans function.

But before scientific knowledge can be aggregated adequately in relation to a problem, the pieces of information basic
to an understanding of the problem must be present. The
strength of a generalization in science can hardly be stronger
than its weakest component. As higher levels of aggregative
generalization have been sought in science, missing pieces of
needed information have often been identified. Known or suspected deficiences in knowledge have sometimes deterred scientists from even attempting generalizations believed, in the
existing state of the art, to be premature (as, for example,
regarding the effect of a 2 percent increase in CO_2 in the
atmosphere).

That the National Environmental Policy Act has forced an
aggregation of scientific knowledge relative to environmental
impacts has been lauded, criticized, and doubted. The act has
sometimes been faulted for forcing assessments of environmental impacts beyond the existing state of scientific knowledge.
But it has also been lauded as, in effect, forcing an identification of the gaps and weaknesses in the existing state of knowledge. Critics argue that, too often, alleged scientific findings
regarding environmental impacts are not soundly based and
that therefore NEPA makes for "bad science." But defenders of

NEPA point out that nothing in the statute induces or excuses "bad science" and that the EIS requirement should not be faulted for deficiencies in the sciences or for misuse of data by incompetent analysts. They argue that identification of what still needs to be known about the behavior of the environment and of natural systems is a positive contribution to the advancement of science that is not likely to be made by concentrating solely on reductionist approaches to the extension of knowledge.

Regardless of how this argument is resolved, it remains that an uncoordinated multidisciplinary approach to understanding complex systemic phenomena is inherently inadequate. Before a coherent picture of reality can emerge, the disparate aggregated information must be integrated. And the integration must be reasonably faithful to the reality of the phenomena observed. This is the purpose expressed through Section 102(2)(a) of NEPA calling for the integrated use of science in decisionmaking.

To summarize, science must be aggregated before it can be integrated—and until it is integrated it can seldom be useful in policymaking. To aggregate science and then to integrate it implies a process of management, although neither scientists nor administrators may perceive the process in managerial terms. "Management of science" is not only management of the funding of research laboratories and scientific projects—it is the management of scientific knowledge itself. For example, an administrator in the Corps of Engineers, the Bureau of Land Management, or the Forest Service, who in cooperation with representatives of relevant disciplines (e.g., through scoping) decides what knowledge is needed in the solution of a problem and determines the particular mix of scientific information that must be brought together in the process of solving the problem, is in effect a manager of science. And as our society moves toward higher levels of information demand, the role of the administrator as a pro forma integrator of scientific knowledge seems certain to increase.

To speak of the integrative function of the administrator is not to suggest single-handed achievement; nor is the integrative function per se something new. The integration and synthesis of diverse factors of many kinds is close to the essence of the administrative function. It always has been a collaborative function in which a particular officer (or group) sometimes is designated as the formal decisionmaker and sometimes is the decisive factor in a collectively developed decision. But the need to integrate scientific (e.g., testable) knowledge into the decision process has been a growing challenge, one less frequently encountered in the simpler past. Political authority today must more often be reconciled with the authority of knowledge. In open democratic societies, where official and scientific information is available to knowledgeable citizens, the policy implications of scientific evidence cannot safely be ignored. Yet, to manage this complex decision process is not easy. It is at least plausible that some of the policy failures in public administration result from the inability of public officials to orchestrate and direct collaborative decisionmaking as well as from individual inability to think in integrative terms.

A tendency strongly marked in American government to promote technical specialists to higher administrative positions may partly account for the fragmentation, contradiction, and instances of excessive zeal or caution that have often characterized government programs. The interdisciplinary team approach of NEPA may diminish these excesses in the future. As science specialists and technicians interact among themselves and with management they may acquire skills and perspectives that the relatively isolated specialists of the past seldom had opportunity to obtain.

The integrative function in environmental decisionmaking assumes two forms. First is integration of scientific and other knowledge into general policy-relevant propositions. Second is coherent focus upon the handling of particular problems to clarify particular issues and translate science-informed propositions into decisionable policy choices. This is a function of administration at many levels in the hierarchies of government. Both aspects of integration are especially needed at those levels of public administration at which basic program decisions occur, and they are clearly indispensable in those divisions of public agencies concerned with the analysis of the impact of agency action on the environment, both natural and social.

In attempting to achieve the integration of diverse sciences moving toward higher levels of generalization, NEPA is undertaking explicitly what other recent statutes have called for by implication. In their planning and decisionmaking, agencies must take account of a variety of protective statutes ranging in subject matter from antiquities to wetlands. Various numbers of these must be considered in any land-use or natural resource management plan. Thus even without NEPA, interaction among specialists to produce coherent policy-focused proposals would be necessary. Similarly, the Principles and Standards for Planning Water and Related Land Resources published and periodically revised by the U.S. Water Resources Council promoted comprehensiveness and integration in project planning. But the process is uneven; under the Reagan administration the future of Principles and Standards is uncertain, possibly to be sacrificed to simplicity in planning.

From Analysis toward Synthesis

The value of a synthesizing use of science is that it may lead to a decisionable set of science-based options or policies upon which policymakers and administrators can act. Before NEPA, agency science tended to be invoked for very specific purposes in multipurpose projects implying multiscience inputs. So-called comprehensive plans in the area of water development were seldom more than composites of the mission-oriented plans of the several agencies pursuing their special programs in the same geographical area, for example, in river basins.

It is not to be inferred that agronomists, entomologists, geologists, hydrologists, and other science specialists in the agencies did not do competent and even distinguished work in their disciplines or that their roles in agency planning were ineffective or counterproductive (although this sometimes may have been the case). Ironically, their technical proficiency often stood in the way of their effective collaboration with other specialists. Promotion ladders in the federal service tended to bring advanced specialists into managerial positions. Planners and decisionmakers too often had no broader perspectives than did their technical subordinates. At worst, the result was one-track linear planning, which was often the cause of inadvertent environmental damage and social miscalculation.

The larger tasks of public administration, however, required synthesis, not only for environmental reasons but for a broad spectrum of economic, social, and political considerations. For this broad view of policy and its applications, public administrators with scientific and technical backgrounds were characteristically poorly prepared. Neither their formal education nor their prior service equipped them to deal with interdisciplinary, interrelating, dynamic problems or to work with persons from unfamiliar fields of expertise in effectively synthesizing diverse inputs into decisionable propositions that could lead to generally effective and sustainable results.

There were often long-standing and close connections between scientist-administrators in government agencies and faculty members in professional schools, notably of agriculture, forestry, mining, civil engineering, and public health. These connections developed naturally because the schools trained specialists to meet the demands of the federal service for specialists. This symbiotic relationship has been a strength in professional higher education and public service in America, but its weakness has lain precisely where environmental policy has required competence—it has not produced effective synthesizers. To have stressed a capacity for synthesis in students preparing to be natural scientists and resource managers would formerly have been to prepare them for job descriptions that did not exist. And in any event, the colleges and the universities were ill-prepared to provide the inter- and multidisciplinary communication that would have been a necessary first step to effect synthesis among those sciences with public policy considerations.

As the environmental movement gained momentum and as public expectations regarding the functions of resource managers changed, many schools began to seek ways to remedy the narrowness of technical and scientific education. As early as 1970, a group of West Coast deans of engineering schools were brought together by the Western Electric Company to consider the educational implications of NEPA and the new environmental policy thrust generally. Conferences on environmental aspects of engineering education were sponsored by the Engineering Foundation. And the environmental movement has influenced professional education in forestry; for example, the Yale School of Forestry was reconstituted as the School of Forestry and Environmental Studies.[3]

In 1969 a survey entitled *Environmental Science Centers at Institutions of Higher Education,* prepared for the House of Representatives Subcommittee on Science, Research, and Development, identified more than two hundred research efforts that were somehow concerned with environmental problems or issues. In 1972 the Commission on Undergraduate Education in the Biological Sciences selected twenty programs of interdisciplinary environmental education to illustrate the variety of academic responses to the emergent environmental concern.[4] These among other inquiries indicated that a rapid and pervasive change was occurring in higher education. But a 1969 study by John S. Steinhart and Stacie Cherniak, undertaken for the president's Science Advisory Committee and entitled *The Universities and the Environment: Commitment to Problem Focused Education,* found that accommodating the new direction of policy to the existing structure of higher education presented difficulties. Not all of the major universities instituted or attempted to undertake environmental programs, and among those that did (e.g., California at Davis, Indiana, Yale, and Wisconsin), very different institutional solutions were adopted. Nevertheless, by the mid-1970s environmental science was clearly built into the structure of American higher education.

It is not that academic deans and federal appointive officials suddenly discovered that skill in synthesis was a needed ingredient in the preparatory education of resource planners and managers. Some of them had previously arrived at this conclusion, but experience with requirements of the environmental impact statement and many new federal and state environmental regulations progressively demonstrated the need for an ability to synthesize as well as analyze. A relatively new way of using science in agency planning was required. Moreover, the parallel development of systems analysis in the public service influenced environmental analysis and planning, facilitating the use of ecosystems concepts, as implicit in Section 102(2)(h) of NEPA. And thus general systems theory, a more generalized aspect of the so-called systems approach to inquiry, joined with ecosystems analysis in pointing toward the need for (and feasibility of) a more syncretic output in agency planning.

But a conceptual trend was occurring and not a generally established condition. Moreover, no claim is made that NEPA per se induced the trend. Systemic interdisciplinary studies such as the 1970 National Academy of Science study of the proposed Kennedy Airport expansion in Jamaica Bay can hardly be attributed to NEPA. What may be claimed, however, is NEPA's role in expanding and reinforcing the idea of a systematic integrative interdisciplinary approach throughout the entire federal bureaucracy and beyond that to policy analysis generally.

Inducing an Environmental Profession

The advancement and proliferation of the sciences, along with new science-based technologies, has had the seemingly contradictory effect of multiplying specialties but blurring professional distinctions. The proliferation of sophisticated high technologies has induced new types of technoscientific professionals. Unlike some fictional scientists, they are not wholly, or mainly, engaged in the pursuit of knowledge for its own sake, although they sometimes do discover new knowledge. Rather, they are the developers, planners, testers, engineers, and managers of knowledge, applying science in a variety of ways to ever-increasing numbers of social and environmental problems.

Some of these new technoscientific environmental professions are merely traditional occupations renamed. The American Academy of Sanitary Engineers became the American Academy of Environmental Engineers; the Federation of Sewage Works Associations became the Water Pollution Control Federation; the Association of Economic Poisons Control Officers became the Association of Pesticide Control Officers; and the Smoke Prevention Association of America became the Air Pollution Control Association. There have also been environmental "retreads" in such professions as forestry, civil engineering, and chemical engineering—the term "environmental" being added to or substituted for a conventional job description. In many professional schools changes in the curricula and postgraduate courses have added an environmental dimension to traditional education. New configurations of expertise may be seen in emerging technoscientific environmental professions. These are more often found in persons trained in the fields of applied ecology, environmental planning, and impact analysis. They are most often identifiable among graduates from universities that grant master of environmental science degrees, and their appearance is a response to opportunities in government and, increasingly, in the private industrial sector.

One reliable indicator of the advance of professionalism in a particular subject matter field is the appearance of new professional associations. NEPA, the pollution control statutes, and a heightened environmental awareness throughout American society have induced formation of a number of occupational groups of which the Association of State and Interstate Water Pollution Control Administrators (1960), the Intersociety Committee on Methods of Air Sampling and Analysis (1962), the National Association for Environmental Education (1971), the National Association of Environmental Professionals (1975), the American Society of Professional Ecologists (1977), and the Society of Power Industry Biologists (1973), among others, illustrate a professionalizing trend.

I believe it is fair to conclude that environmental legislation in general, and NEPA in particular, have influenced the scope, content, and direction of science, and in so doing have begun to induce new science occupations. A public need for science-informed managers of environmental policy and a corresponding need in the regulated private sector for environmentally competent specialists have created an employment demand for persons trained in various aspects of the environmental sciences. In general, but with some aloofness in the traditional disciplines, academic response has included changes in the traditional curricula in the sciences and has led to the establishment of new schools, departments, and programs to prepare people for the responsibilities that legislation like NEPA demands. Linkages between educational institutions and administrative agencies that have been well known in agriculture, forestry, civil engineering, and many other science-related fields are now becoming evident in the broader and more complex field of environmental policy and management.

The term "scientist" is becoming less descriptive—less meaningful—as these proliferating, ramifying, and synthesizing trends continue. And they are evident in science-related fields other than the environmental, notably in biomedicine, electronics, and communications. It is beside the point to argue that engineering is being confused with science and that applied sciences (which some purists do not regard as science at all) threaten to adulterate true, basic scientific inquiry. All this may be true; but it is more significantly true that as science in the several senses used in this book continues to expand, it tends to lose the sharpness of its traditional distinctions. For many science-related positions today, it might be more accurate to discard the term "scientist" as no longer indicative of a well-defined occupation and simply use the more comprehensive term "science professional."

With specific reference to the environment, Lee Hannah of the Department of Environmental Science and Engineering at the University of California at Los Angeles calls for "a new breed of environmental professionals, professionals committed to environmental quality and able to work realistically with industry, able to understand and analyze complex issues spanning multiple disciplines, and able to initiate and facilitate meaningful forums on environmental problems."[5]

A Megascience of Environment?

Is environmental science mostly a figure of speech or do we in fact have an emerging science of the environment with distinctive method, theory, and content? A definitive answer to this question may be premature, but the presence of courses, programs, schools, and professorships in environmental science indicates that at least some significant sector of the community of science and higher education believes that it is not improper to speak of such a science.

One might with equal propriety speak of a hypothetical "megascience of the environment," which would be a large and inclusive syncretic science including substantial parts of others. Or one might speak of a "metascience"—a new form extending beyond the boundaries of conventional science. Both designations, although unconventional, are nevertheless appropriate because environmental science comprises or is based upon a vast array of physical, biological, and even social sciences. It extends beyond the present boundaries of science (as some persons would define them) partly because it employs and needs to discover new syncretic methodologies that will increase our understanding of how the natural systems of the world work. And, in common with many aspects of the biological and social sciences, it impinges on fields such as ethics and aesthetics, which are generally believed to lie beyond the purview of science or at least of the so-called "scientific method" narrowly defined.

It seems clear that if a megascience of the environment must be both aggregative and integrative, a suitable methodology must also be developed to accomplish this process and to provide coherent and intelligible propositions and models to which decisionmakers may have recourse in endeavoring to determine which of the available alternatives toward solving a policy problem is likely to be optimal, given the total situation. If this appears to suggest that the hypothetical rational decision-maker is being revisited, the impression is only partially correct. Unlike the uses of science to set standards in pollution control or safety standards, science in NEPA is intended to persuade the planner and administrator to scan the field of action before acting. A megascience of environmental relationships, effectively used, could greatly assist agencies and their administrators to overcome the tyranny of small decisions—to break the incremental chain of decisionmaking that may lead toward environmentally unwanted consequences.

This is why simulation and modeling of environmental phenomena and of environment-impacting processes can be valuable aids to decisionmakers. In theory at least, a well-developed comprehensive model integrates the components of an environmental situation and results in a synthesis that can make explicit the range of possibilities faced in an environment-affecting decision. Models, of course, are simulations of reality and not reality itself; they are simplifications of whole systems, and they sometimes omit aspects important to policy decisions. Models may be very good at detailing the actual physical processes occurring in the environment, but they may not be effective in revealing the implications of those processes or human reactions to them, especially the intensity with which those reactions are experienced. An exclusively quantifying systems methodology probably cannot provide an adequate base for a megascience of the environment, although it may afford a very substantial part of the foundation.

Traditional historical-institutional studies and more sophisticated in-depth case studies are also needed to reveal what the more quantitative simulations and system studies are likely to leave out. A syncretic science of the environment cannot therefore be defined by methodology except and insofar as it must employ methods that assist the integrating and synthesizing of aggregated essential scientific knowledge.

We do not have an informative model of environmental science, although I once proposed an effort to build one. Some years ago, I suggested the construction of a hierarchy of environmental knowledge that would indicate interrelationships among the many components of that knowledge and would reveal gaps and weak places in its structure. The proposition did not arouse interest. Were I convinced that it was infeasible I would abandon it; I may be mistaken, but I am not yet persuaded that the project would not be doable, or that when completed it would not be useful.

We do not yet know all we need to know about how to identify the problems to be researched in environmental science; nor is the stage of our knowledge often sufficient for us to defend our chosen priorities in research on grounds other than personal interest or the availability of funding. If some part of the effort that has been expended on costly environmental games and simulations were to have been devoted to constructing a hierarchical representation of environmental science, I believe that the payoff from subsequently funded research might have been considerably increased. Even if the hierarchical model did not prove constructible, it is possible that the effort to build it would prove rich in serendipity. But given the seeming priorities of most scientists and funders of research, I think it unlikely that such a modeling of the state of environmental science will be undertaken in the near future.

Impressive as the growth of environmental studies has been, it is nevertheless questionable whether the extent of support—especially for research—is adequate to the need. This assessment of need is measured by the apparent worsening of such dangerous trends as loss of topsoil, increasing CO_2 and acidification of the atmosphere, and extinctions of species. Here there has been no dearth of high-level prestigious advocates of a major national and international research effort, but all but one proposal have come to nothing. The exception (although an uncertain one) has been The Institute of Ecology (TIE), because it was actually established. But it was exceptional in a second respect that may have contributed to its limited success. Unlike the others, TIE had no politically or financially powerful sponsors. Its sponsors were chiefly working scientists in universities, museums, and government laboratories. Assisted by a relatively modest grant from the National Science

Foundation, its founding was largely the work of unpaid volunteers. Its existence has been precarious, but it has survived into the 1980s.

The history of the other efforts is a chronology of the short life expectancy of great ideas. If it is surprising that a group of environmental scientists with no real money and little experience in institution building brought off TIE, it should be astonishing that propositions supported by the power and prestige of the White House, the National Science Foundation, members of the National Academy of Sciences, influential members of the United States Congress, the Ford Foundation, the Aspen Institute, and the Mitre Corporation never got off the ground.

Between 1971 and 1976 at least six institutional arrangements were proposed for advancing policy-oriented environmental research. At least three of these reached the stage of bills introduced into the United States Congress, among the more interesting being the proposal endorsed by President Richard Nixon in his 1971 environmental message (mentioned in Chapter 3).[6] Supported by the CEQ, the NSF, and the Ford Foundation and with substantial funding almost in hand, the proposal was suddenly aborted, ostensibly because of disagreement among White House staff over the selection of its director. But the explanation that the environmental institute was never established "because of difficulties in finding the right person" to direct it suggests a lack of perseverance among its sponsors that can most plausibly be attributed to a lack of real commitment. But if the idea was ever worth pursuing to the extent of a presidential message and a bill in the Congress, why was it not worth following through? Report has it that only one candidate was ever considered for the directorship and he was rejected on grounds irrelevant to the assignment.

In 1973 the institute idea was revived by executives of the Mitre Corporation and influential scientist-administrators associated with the National Center for Atmospheric Research. Cautiously described as the XYZ Institute, it came to no more than a substantial investment of time by a group of well-qualified and well-placed individuals who knew how to get things done.

Environmental issues have figured prominently in the work of the more substantively inclusive but more specifically methodological International Institute of Applied Systems Analysis (IIASA) in Austria.[7] Some of the same impetus behind the several institutes proposed in the United States contributed to the establishment of the IIASA. Many of its published studies evidenced a search for synthesis, usually through quantitative methodologies. Yet as of 1981 the future of IIASA was uncertain, in part perhaps because of that same skepticism as to usefulness that stood in the way of comparable efforts in America.

An apparent regional success that should not be overlooked is the Environment and Policy Institute of the East-West Center in Honolulu, established in 1977. Contrary to what almost all informed people believed at the time of the United Nations Conference on the Human Environment in 1972, the NEPA idea has spread abroad and is being taken seriously (at least in concept) in much of South and Southeast Asia, among other places. The East-West Center, funded largely through congressional appropriations, has been carrying on genuine interdisciplinary policy-relevant research in a cross-cultural setting. There is some reason to believe that adoption of the EIS procedures and associated uses of scientific analytic methods are effecting changes in the governments and educational institutions of several Asian countries that a decade ago would have been unbelievable.

There must be some impetus behind an idea that, although repeatedly submerged, continues to surface. Thomas Kuhn's theory of *The Structure of Scientific Revolutions* (1962) may be relevant to this circumstance. There is without doubt a core of opposition to the research approach implicit in the interdisciplinary institute idea. Reductionist, discipline-bound research is still widely regarded as the only legitimate science. Moreover, there may be some tactical opposition within the National Academy of Science and National Science Foundation toward potential new participants in setting agendas for scientific research. In addition, a policy-oriented institute logically calls for the involvement of social scientists, a prospect distasteful to some self-styled "hard" scientists. The proposal of Senator Fred Harris of Oklahoma to establish a National Social Science Foundation was not well received, even by some scientists who thought that the social sciences had no proper place in the NSF. If this sense of territoriality has had any significance on national policy, it may also have affected the inability of the CEQ to fulfill its mandate under Title II of NEPA to promote environmental research.

The social science problem is the more troublesome because there is no single well-defined peer group through which social scientists appropriate to the tasks of environmental policy research can be identified. Some peer group formation may be occurring at an embryonic stage. Among sociologists there is a social impact assessment network; there are associations of environmental economists and historians and an environmental policy subgroup in the Policy Studies Association. Environmental lawyers were drawn together as a group by the opportunities and demands of environmental litigation for which NEPA has received perhaps more than its share of credit. There is a small network of political scientists interested in environmental politics although their discipline has perhaps been the least responsive of the social sciences to environmental concerns.

Does this account of some qualified successes and several well-launched failures tell us anything regarding the feedback of environmental policy upon science? I believe that it tells us, first, that our policy commitments signalized by NEPA require a form of scientific inquiry that our present institutions have not yet provided (at least to the extent needed); second, that although our establishment leadership in government, science, and the foundations recognizes the need (reluctantly), it is uncertain as to how the need should be met; third, that the preponderant opinion among this leadership (including many of its leading scientists) is that environmental policy problems will yield to technical answers; and fourth, that unless an environmental policy institute can be staffed at the outset by persons meeting establishment credibility tests (a small field for recruitment) nothing can be done. But all this merely demonstrates that conceptual and institutional innovation is difficult and normally protracted even when attempted by persons of sincerity, intelligence, and foresight.

The foregoing discussion records both conjecture and failure regarding the possibility of achieving a new level of integration among the sciences. Although the history of science has demonstrated the reality of an integrative as well as a proliferative growth, it is difficult to show convincingly that a new level of synthesis has emerged when the evidence for it is no more than circumstantial. Direct experience wiith the Bureau of Land Management, the Forest Service, and the Corps of Engineers persuades me that NEPA has influenced these agencies to attempt an integrated interdisciplinary use of science in planning. In personal interviews I have found as typical the remarks of Bob Leopold, chief of the Division of Planning and Coordination, BLM Colorado: "We have tried to stress interdisciplinary work rather than multidisciplinary work.... When we do an environmental statement we very much stress the interdisciplinary function."[8] Similarly, Larry J. Lower, chief of environmental resources of the Baltimore District, Corps of Engineers, says, "We have an interdisciplinary team approach to all planning studies."[9] The conclusion that an integrated interdisciplinary approach is being attempted in a large number of offices and agencies appears justified by more comprehensive studies not yet published.[10]

In conformity with the requirements of NEPA and its regulations, teams of science professionals with varying degrees of specialization have been collectively developing approaches to integrated impact assessment that university science specialists almost never have had occasion to attempt. The Passaic River Basin Study Group in the New York District of the Corps of Engineers is one example of an interdisciplinary team attacking a complex problem over a period of years. The California Desert Plan and impact statement project, as previously noted, is another and one of the more elaborate examples.

For most of such efforts it would be unreasonable to expect initial or complete success. But for the larger, more complex issues the team approach is becoming standard procedure. They represent a kind of on-the-job learning for which previous academic training has been largely and until recently nonexistent. There is, moreover, substantial skepticism, especially in academia, that a new level of integration among the sciences is producing—or will ever produce—a megascience of environmental relationships. The skeptics may be right, although I read the history of science and the circumstantial evidence as pointing toward the ultimate consolidation of an inclusive environmental science that will enable policymakers to arrive at more sustainable and less risky choices than are possible today. And more than any other public event NEPA has by implication moved science toward this development.

If an integrated level of environmental science cannot be achieved, significant improvements in the uses of science in planning and policymaking will nevertheless have been made. But a ceiling or limit will also have been encountered, blocking further advancement of science in this area. A real and tangible limit to growth will have been encountered—a limit inherent in the human mind. Serious questions would arise—and should already have arisen as a precautionary strategy—as to the extent of human ability to take over from nature the management of large, complex ecosystems. Has human ingenuity risen to its level of incompetence? The question should be troubling to advocates of unlimited growth who regard the goals and methods of NEPA as reflecting an obstructive, impractical idealism.

This question might be evaded by distinguishing programmatic synthesis, which is what NEPA seeks, from intellectual synthesis, which would be a new level of perception or understanding achieved through the interaction of various disciplines. It is possible to integrate or synthesize the inputs of different specialists into a comprehensive plan, and the result might be called programmatic synthesis. More often in actuality the result has been a multidisciplinary montage. This has been a frequent consequence of interagency planning when jurisdictional and mission protectiveness adds to disciplinary exclusiveness. To achieve a true synthesis in substance some degree of intellectual synthesis seems necessary.

In some federal offices and agencies it appears that an approach to intellectual synthesis has been occurring among members of environmental analysis and planning teams. In the development of environmental assessments and impact statements, mutual learning occurs among many individuals whose prior education has been specialized. Although not all offices and not all persons respond to this opportunity for cross-disciplinary learning, many do. The result is a growth in the number of interdisciplinary people who can synthesize information and ideas intellectually as well as in a composite plan. To the extent that such people contribute to the NEPA process, the result should be more effective programmatic synthesis and reorientation of the process by which policy decisions have traditionally been made.

6
Managing Science in Policy and Administration

Both the great achievements and the man-made disasters of the recent past have been related to the way science has been used. Our success in coping with the problems our society has created for itself, and possibly even the survival of society, depend upon making a better and different use of science in the future than in the past. To manage policy and administration more effectively through reliance upon science, science must first be managed to produce results (1) in the right amount, (2) in the right form, (3) at the right place, and (4) at the right time.

This is not to say that *all* science ought to be managed. A large part of scientific research is managed, however, through controls implicit in the programming, reviewing, and funding of research. For the greater part of science today for which laboratories, equipment, personnel, and predictable resources are necessary, the question regarding management is not "whether," but "what kind." For those aspects of science bearing directly upon public policies, there seems little justification for leaving scientific investigation to chance. With respect to large and complex problems of the environment, scientific work for which no organizational and financial provisions are made is work that cannot be undertaken.

The Science-Policy Relationship

Science, placed at the service of policy, is subsequently shaped by the needs of policy; but science and political authority, whether secular or ecclesiastic, have never been comfortable associates. Authority in science is testable knowledge, subject to change with very little notice. Authority in government is based upon cultural norms for which the validity tests of science are largely irrelevant. Authoritarian societies of both the right and the left have been unable consistently to reconcile science with ideology. Nor have democratic societies always found this an easy task. To democratic politicians, the voice of the people may be the voice of God, but scientists may question whether "the people" have really understood the message or whether the politician is a reliable interpreter.

Historically, "science" as knowledge and method has not consistently been used "scientifically"; the use of science has seldom been guided by scientific principles. The expansion of science and of the demands that societies have made upon science have increased the occasions for incompatibilities to arise. Science may be very accommodating in helping society to obtain the things that it is alleged to want, but then it may be importunate in telling society things that not everyone wants to know. Science as an enterprise in the service of society has not been in a good position to guide its own development or to assess its priorities through recourse to its own principles. Science as an obedient servant is not called upon to produce embarrassing knowledge. But if the needs of society require knowledge that conventional science cannot provide, and if the knowledge applied turns out to have undesired consequences, society may require a more "scientific" approach to basic research as well as to application.

Thus we are back to the Baconian dictum that "nature to be commanded must be obeyed." But nature to be obeyed must be understood, and hence modern governments, aware of growing problems in the environment, face the practical necessity of encouraging the development of a more comprehensive policy-oriented environmental science. Yet in so doing they find it difficult to avoid subsidizing the production of knowledge that influential groups may find politically objectionable. Nevertheless, the most hardheaded antienvironmentalist will also find it difficult to deny such relief as science may bring to citizens frightened by the proximity of lethal chemical dumps, or to be ungrateful to environmental scientists who might find some way to deactivate or to safely employ radioactive residues from nuclear generating plants.

Environmentalism may not be a welcome addition to the troubles of politicians, but it is not likely to go away without the assistance of environmental science. Until modern society learns how to establish a conserving and sustainable relationship with its environment, political expressions of concern for the state of the environment are almost certain to continue. As long as there is an apparent verifiable, measurable deterioration in the quality of the human environment, there will be a politics of the environment, and environmental science will be invoked to resolve political controversy.

Managing Science through NEPA

The environmental impact statement, as I have previously emphasized, is a procedural tool of policy using science to achieve the goals of the National Environmental Policy Act through planning and public administration. The essence of the EIS process is the application of science (as contrasted with guesswork) to ascertain the environmental impacts of government actions. The process begins with analyses, carries on through the aggregation and collation of data, to integration into a coherent input into decisionmaking.

Unlike changes of the seasons, the NEPA process does not occur naturally—it must be managed. But some critics of the uses of science will nevertheless protest that the management of science—of knowledge—is something that we do not want public officials to do. The facts, they say, should speak for themselves; yet in reality the "facts" are silent—someone always speaks for the facts, and they are often susceptible to more than one interpretation. The application of scientific knowledge to any problem requires judgment as to what facts are relevant and reliable. Critics of the uses of science in government point out that the management of research and of information is certain to be selective and hence susceptible to abuse—to improper and bureaucratic advantage. Evidence does not demonstrate that scientists, many of whom are highly specialized, are better informed regarding the state of knowledge generally and are more objective and broad-minded interpreters of the public interest than are many nonscientists. The management of information for the public good is a major concern for present-day societies in which information is a more powerful force than ever before. How much public understanding of science is needed for the responsible use of science by government (or by the private sector) is not easily ascertained.

The extent to which science can (or should) be "managed" in the sense of political determination of methods and priorities is certainly subject to debate. But the critical position of science in modern society now makes this debate inevitable.[1]

There are at least two reasons why we should be concerned with the management of scientific knowledge in government. The first is because we have evolved a society so complex and so dependent upon high levels of information that management of knowledge is needed in order to avoid man-made disasters resulting from conflicting interests and from the unforeseen consequences of unexamined actions. The second reason for concern is that bureaucrats and technocrats will manage knowledge anyway. They have done so in the past and will continue as long as society requires government. As science grows in scope and power, it becomes all the more important that it be guided in the public interest. But how?

The nature of the "public interest" has been debated for as long as politics has existed. The most that can be said about it here is that the public interest within the context of public environmental policy is not always self-evident. If it exists, it may be discovered through experience, but this has often proved costly in life, values, and property. The EIS requirement of NEPA substitutes scientific inquiry for trial and possible error. To the extent that it is effective, it spares society the cost of unforeseen consequences. But this advantage cannot be obtained without a price. The price of environmental impact analysis may be far less in many respects than the cost of environmental error, but the price of the former is seldom directly comparable to the costs of the latter. And whatever the costs, they are allocated differently.

The ability of modern society to dispense with informed environmental management has declined as rapidly as the power of science and technology has increased. A relatively decentralized, self-directive society may be possible and indeed has been advocated by persons who speak of steady states and indefinitely sustainable social orders. Yet even in these circumstances, privately directed scientific innovations might raise serious problems. Nevertheless, science is absolutely needed to keep the present society going—to compensate for its diminishing assets and to help society avoid destroying its environment. Science may be necessary to enable humanity to avoid destroying itself.

NEPA provides the administrative agencies of government with an obligation and an opportunity to mobilize the science needed to cope with a large sector of public problems. But science does not perform this service automatically, nor do all sciences contribute equally to social necessities. Misuse of science in relation to the environment has contributed to many difficulties in the past and unfortunately continues to do so. Health, safety, economic welfare, and happiness have been impaired. What has been needed is a way not only to deploy scientific knowledge in a manner that will serve the public interest, but also to discover criteria for the public interest upon which almost everyone can, in principle, agree.

Throughout the 1960s and into the 1970s, debate over priorities in scientific research and development was vigorous and often rancorous. It began with controversy over nuclear weapons and the role of the military-industrial complex and, adding new areas of contention, focused in the middle 1970s upon developments in biology, notably on the issue of genetic engineering and experiments with recombinant DNA.[2] For the most part, the arguments were negative, stressing what government-supported science should not do. More sober appraisals of what government should do in relation to science were often lost in the contention.

In a 1966 report, *Environmental Pollution: A Challenge to Science and Technology,* a congressional committee found that "federal government scientific activities are not yet channeled to support announced goals in pollution abatement" and observed that "ecology, as an organized profession, is not in good condition to become the umbrella for increased research."[3] A decade later, and six years after NEPA had become an official expression of national goals and priorities, Richard Carpenter, a leading student of the scientific basis of the act, declared, "Just as science is important to NEPA, the Act has implications for science that have not been exploited.... The more comprehensive ecosystem studies have not been well supported."[4] The authorization under Title II of NEPA for the CEQ "to conduct investigations, studies, surveys, research, and analyses relating to ecological systems and environmental quality" was never implemented, and the function was transferred under Reorganization Plan 3 of 1970 to the Environmental Protection Agency, where it has largely languished. Thus, although the need to develop a science adequate to support declared policy has been recognized and reiterated, public support adequate to meet the need has not been forthcoming. Nevertheless, the scientific capabilities that are needed to achieve the goals of NEPA have in partial and unsystematic ways been forced by the exigencies of the act itself.

In a study on the political economy of land-use policy, James C. Hite correctly identifies the reformist consequences of NEPA. They are found in the obstacles that NEPA raises to the self-serving use of science by government agencies and their clients. But he is less correct in his interpretation of the way this effect has been accomplished. He writes, "The NEPA requirement for maximum public input disrupts the cozy relationship between the business community and government bureaucrats."[5] NEPA has indeed disrupted long-standing government-client relationships, but not because of a requirement for maximum public input. There is no such requirement in NEPA.

NEPA does provide an opportunity for public input through comment on draft environmental impact statements. Through the EIS procedures, NEPA compels the agencies to disclose publicly significant elements in their planning and decision process. Such disclosure enables representatives of the public to intervene provided that they conform to judicial rules regarding public interest lawsuits. Effective challenge requires that the EIS can be shown to be inadequate in substance, or that its preparation has been inconsistent with strictures of procedural law, or that the proposed action that it discloses can be found by the courts to be in contravention of the intent of Congress as expressed in the act. Government agencies, moreover, possess a number of long-established technical legal defenses to prevent the courts from substituting judicial for administrative interpretations of the public interest. An agency may fend off judicial interference if it can establish that the form of its proposed action is discretionary and not mandatory or that its responsibility in the issue is proprietary and not ministerial. NEPA provides a key, but by no means guarantees an open door to public interposition in agency decisionmaking.

Thus it is not merely the opportunity for public participation in the decision process that gives NEPA its power; the strength of NEPA is rather to be found in the mandatory substantive provisions of the act regarding the uses of science in planning and decisionmaking. NEPA not only imposes certain obligations upon planners and decisionmakers; it also provides a rationale and legitimization of adequately considered decisionmaking that many public officials welcome. There is no justification for assuming that public officials are indifferent to the quality of their decisions.

NEPA, by implication, also imposes requirements upon citizens who would use its provisions to counter or to correct administrative policy. Only to the extent that citizen protesters and their legal counsel understand science well enough to draw out its implications for particular issues are they in a position to challenge the adequacy of authenticity of agencies' environmental impact statements. Thus, before the public effectively attacks the uses of science by government agencies, it must first do its homework with respect to the sciences relevant to the issues in dispute.

Does Better Science Equal Better Management?

But can we be sure that the science requirements of NEPA have in fact resulted in management decisions consistent with the policies declared in the act, and is there any evidence that the uses of science as mandated in Section 102 do in fact lead toward a science more adequate to the needs of environmental management? Simple yes, no, or maybe answers are not feasible. Meaningful answers must be qualified, if for no other reason than that the questions themselves imply judgments regarding quality or value.

Such evidence as we have of the NEPA-science-management relationship suggests a positive answer. If the goals stated in NEPA are taken as criteria for evaluating the environmental performance of management, then it seems safe to conclude that NEPA has in fact resulted in better management. Public projects are being undertaken with much greater sensitivity to environmental effects, and the informational basis of planning is more adequate. Testimony from government planners and managers whose experience precedes NEPA weighs heavily in favor of NEPA as a constructive and needed factor in agency planning and decisionmaking. On many occasions, administrators in different agencies and in different parts of the country have remarked to me that the broadened basis of agency competence resulting from the NEPA-mandated interdisciplinary use of science has greatly improved the quality of agency planning and decisionmaking.

This judgment must be qualified by recognizing that, as yet, the full potential of NEPA for science and for management has not been realized. The fault here is not with the act but with the failure of the Congress and the executive fully to implement its provisions. Reinforcement of NEPA by Executive Order 11991 of 24 May 1977, directing the CEQ to issue procedural regulations, formalized a major step toward better management. After a decade of experience, many of the more difficult and troublesome aspects of the administration of NEPA have been overcome. Yet the quality of planning and decisionmaking is still limited by the adequacy of the knowledge base.

During the first decade of NEPA, the scientific foundation for environmental administration was broadened and strengthened, in significant measure owing to the EIS requirements of the act. But in relation to NEPA's goals and mandates, the scientific foundation remains inadequate. Research priorities tend to be set by political exigencies, as in the acid rain issue, rather than by a systematic interdisciplinary inquiry leading toward illumination of the Sections 201 and 204 authorizations regarding "the status and condition of the major natural, manmade, or altered environmental classes" and "current and foreseeable trends." The *Global 2000* report of 1980 may be regarded as a belated response to NEPA, but a continuing and not merely a onetime assessment is what ecological realities require.[6]

The drafters of NEPA realized that achievement of its goals would require time. It was a policy act for the long term, not a regulatory measure to change orientation immediately on enactment, although certain procedural changes were at once required. Anyone familiar with bureaucratic behavior knows that policies and procedures can be manipulated and that a substantial lead time measured in years is normally necessary to transform ingrained practices in human institutions.

What is lead time for policy reformers is often lag time for government agencies. Only the naive should therefore be surprised that, after ten years of NEPA, public works extravaganzas of such dubious merit environmentally and economically as the Garrison Diversion and the Central Arizona projects were still seriously contemplated by the United States government. Nor should it be surprising that government and industry have been planning more technological developments for the Rocky Mountain area than some experts believe the available water sources may be able to supply. Residuals of past perceptions and plans carry over into the present. As the histories of reevaluation and reform continue to demonstrate, time is necessary to effect change in human society. When, for example, a need for reorientation was perceived within the U.S. Army Corps of Engineers and Chief of Engineers General Frederick Clark in 1970 invited an environmental advisory board to help him "turn this monster around," neither he nor the board believed that the turnaround could take place overnight. Thus, in assessing the impact of NEPA on public administration and the corresponding impact of the demands of administration upon science to fulfill the requirements of the act, regard should be given to the time normally required for major institutional change.

From no part of the preceding discussion should it have been inferred that all acts of federal agencies that affect the environment are harmful. Many indeed are beneficial or neutral in effect; many are in some respects simultaneously helpful and harmful. One might assume that changes in public plans or policies resulting from scientific information developed through environmental impact analysis would in fact result in better management decisions. This would, of course, be a normative judgment and dependent upon criteria for ascertaining what is "better." The significance of such assessment depends upon being able to link the proposed criteria for quality with evidence of administrative change.

It is impossible to quantify all of the agency proposals that have been modified and the number that have been abandoned as a result of the NEPA process. Most proposals are now developed with the requirements of NEPA in mind, lessening the probability of subsequent modification or rejection. A balance sheet would have to include environmental assessments—preliminary reviews of proposals that may eliminate obviously unacceptable projects or result in their substantial revision before they ever reach the EIS stage. Such reviews may also remove from further environmental impact analysis proposals having no significant relevance. No doubt many ideas for actions with environmentally damaging consequences that once would have been seen through to completion now do not even receive serious consideration because of NEPA. The better the letter and spirit of the substantive provisions of NEPA are implemented, the more difficult it becomes to ascertain precisely the effects of the act.

Changes in agency action resulting from environmental assessment or impact analysis may be accounted, generally, as improvements. But because NEPA is not the only statute affecting administrative decisionmaking, and because planners and administrators may develop an environmental awareness independent of the NEPA mandates, and for other reasons, it may be inaccurate to attribute improvements in environment-related planning and decisionmaking to NEPA exclusively. Yet testimony in congressional oversight hearings, evaluations by observers independent of agency influence, and empirical evidence linking the EIS process with revision or cancellation of agency action support the inference that NEPA has had a positive influence upon the administrative process. But rather than attempting to determine just how constructive NEPA has been, it may be more productive to examine the obstacles to more effective uses of science in environmental policymaking and planning. There is evidence to support at least two lines of improvement.

The first line is organizational: building environmental analysis and synthesis into the planning and programming parts of the agency. The second line is informational. In implementing NEPA the tendency, as has been noted, has been to create new and separate offices for environmental impact analysis. In some agencies, where there was little environmental awareness among personnel and pronounced professional resistance to the EIS process, this separate status may have been advantageous in effecting NEPA goals. A separate environmental capability may have been necessary until the balance of the organization could be brought into line with NEPA goals and values.

The disadvantage of the separate organizational status is that, insofar as it is out of the mainline planning and decisionmaking structure of an agency, an environmental analysis unit's findings might be more easily ignored. The mutual educational value of its closer interaction with other decisions in the agency would not be obtained. But on the other hand, to incorporate the environmental analysis function within an unsympathetic or unprepared agency might be to lose its effectiveness in the "business as usual" activities of the agency. If an agency is not prepared to take the NEPA mandate seriously, it may not matter greatly how the environmental impact analysis function is structured. But if slowness of agency compliance is primarily attributable to bureaucratic inertia or inexperience, then the way the impact analysis function is built into the agency may be significant to agency performance in relation to the environmental impact of its policies and programs. In a word, the most practical consideration in initial organization for environmental impact analysis would appear to be circumstance.

Over the years, however, it appears that in many agencies—notably those engaged in large-scale natural resource management—the NEPA function is not isolated and has increasingly become an integral part of the operations of the agency. Although planning and environmental units are formally distinguished in some agencies, they characteristically work under the leadership of a coordinator who is in fact the responsible administrator for the joint functioning of both units.

During the Carter administration, the enhanced role of the Council on Environmental Quality in promulgating regulations (as distinguished from guidelines) for the environmental impact statement process appears to have been a major step toward more effective use of science and agency decisions more attuned to NEPA goals. Certainly, departmental experience and the implementation of the CEQ regulations have markedly improved the technical aspects of the NEPA process.

These improvements have been notable in shortening impact statements, in focusing on the essential aspects of environmental impact, and in such procedures as tiering and scoping, which in the long run conserve both time and money in obtaining better environmental decisions. Complaints that NEPA procedures are costly should be taken seriously only after comparison is made with the costs of litigation intended to correct or stop environmentally insensitive or destructive agency action. And, more important, the costs should also be compared with the costs of making serious environmental mistakes, even when those costs are not borne immediately by society but may accrue over many years to be paid by future generations.

These technical measures lead to the second major line of improvement in the NEPA process: development of more effective means to aggregate and integrate science into the decision process. The task here is one of information management. There is no costless way of managing man's relationships with his environment, but investments in information, made at an opportune time, might pay off manyfold over the long run. An example of such an investment would be the development of data banks and retrieval systems that could be drawn upon in the preparation of future analyses and would act as benchmarks to permit comparative monitoring of environmental change and follow-up testing of the effectiveness of environmental impact analyses.[7]

There are serious obstacles to the effective utilization of large and comprehensive data systems. Yet there would be many advantages in knowing how different agencies or divisions within the same agency had addressed similar environmental problems. At present, such information is obtainable largely in an informal ad hoc manner, based heavily on personal contacts. In the Bureau of Land Management, however, a promising innovation has been proposed in the form of an "experience bank." This would not be a comprehensive data base; it would instead provide a full text storage and retrieval capability for records of decision. Rather than focusing on past impact statements per se, Bruce L. Bandurski, National Environmental Policy Act Officer in BLM, believes that

> it would make sense to work backwards from what the decision-makers have relied on in the way of information for the decision-making, to have full text coverage of what the record of decision says about the consideration that was given to the various alternatives, the rationale for choosing the one that was chosen, what mitigating measures were proposed, what predictions were made that we ought to be following up with monitoring on the ground, and have a feedback loop that brings some realism to this process and not allow the process to be essentially cut off at the time the statement is filed and put on the shelf.[8]

This concept of monitoring, follow-up, and feedback would extend the EIS beyond a cautionary or action-forcing device to a continuing tool of management and evaluation. The full decision record and the feedback loop would assist an agency to assess the accuracy of its predictions, to see how mitigation measures have been working, and to adapt subsequent decisions as feedback may indicate. This concept of the EIS as a tool of active management is shared by practitioners in the field. Elwin Price, chief of the Division of Planning and Environmental Coordination of the BLM in Wyoming, observes that "the bureau exists to manage things, not to write documents." He declares that "no matter how many EISs we are writing, if we are not translating the EIS into decisions, management, and the use of these lands, we have failed."[9]

Building impact analysis into an active management process is exactly what NEPA was intended to accomplish and would make the EIS a true decision document and not merely a ritualistic report. After reviewing the fate of one hundred projects for which EISs were filed in 1973, a Columbia University research team concluded that, generally, "the EIS does appear to be integrated into the decisionmaking process."[10] In their final report, the Columbia University investigators observed that "as a consequence of the NEPA review procedure" science-related comments caused changes to be made in the final EIS and sometimes in the project.[11]

It is not inconsistent with the Columbia findings or the thesis of this book to conclude that the uses of science in the EIS process have been improving and are generally resulting in more environmentally defensible decisions, even though the quality of scientific information and to some extent of method may not have significantly improved. It is not easy to devise a test for determining how much improvement in the scientific content of the EIS generally can be declared "significant."

It is easier to establish the increased use of science, whatever its quality, in decisionmaking than to evaluate the quality of science in an EIS. The quality of science has some relationship to the purpose for which it is used; quality of particular scientific findings in the abstract is a largely theoretical concept over which experts may differ. In assessing the scientific merits of a policy decision, the quality of integrated scientific findings in an EIS may be greater than the "pure science" quality of specific disciplinary inputs. Not only are the true tests of quality different for different purposes, such as "quality in what sense?" but contributions from some fields of science to the aggregate product may offset inadequacies in others.

The EIS process has revealed areas in which the state of science is deficient. But neither the Congress nor the private sector has made investments in scientific knowledge and technology sufficient to justify an expectation that the content of science in the EIS would improve rapidly. I believe that the science content in EISs has shown significant improvement selectively, but for a strongly marked general increase, attention must be given to the state of science. Agency procedures cannot fully address all environmental issues that might be relevant to a particular decision, especially those involving large ecosystems and the responsibilities of numerous agencies and jurisdictions over time. There is need for comprehensive in-depth policy-oriented environmental research that would consider alternative policies in relation to particular issues, not merely what was proposed, and to provide an independent review of the EIS process. One means to this end could be case studies that would distill general trends, behaviors, and principles from the record of public experience. Research, independent of agency sponsorship, could be undertaken in anticipation of emerging environmental controversies. This would have the advantage of examining an issue before pressures are generated by proposed agency action. The CEQ has legal authority to support such inquiry but has rarely attempted to do so.

The research approaches most persuasive at the present time appear to be technique-oriented quantitative simulations and modeling exercises that sometimes have the superficial appearance of being more "scientific" than traditional historical-institutional research methods. Both approaches are necessary. Technical methods may improve the quality of impact statement analysis, but there are few wholly technical solutions to the problems of environmental policy where the components are large, numerous, and complex.

Full realization of the potential of NEPA depends upon the priorities of the president and upon the way he interprets his constitutional responsibility to take care that the law be faithfully executed. The judiciary has been reluctant and ambivalent in affirming the substantive mandate of NEPA. The courts have not agreed that Section 101—the Declaration of National Environmental Policy—is substantively enforceable with respect to the agencies, but in this respect the president has constitutional authority to do what the courts will not do, and a variety of means are available to do it, notably through the powers to budget, to appoint, to reorganize, and to adopt programs. The president, moreover, has his "bully pulpit," as Theodore Roosevelt put it, that enables a skilled political leader to persuade public opinion. The president could, of course, use the authority granted by Title II of NEPA to extend and upgrade scientific knowledge relative to the goals of the act. But no president has thus far shown interest in doing so.

From a twenty-first-century retrospect, the National Environmental Policy Act may very possibly be seen as one of the more significant pieces of legislation to have been enacted by a United States Congress. This statement may not be hyperbole or an exaggeration if NEPA proves to have signalized a major change of course in American society toward a less destructive, more conserving economy. A leading student of environmental law has written: "NEPA has developed into a successful tool for compelling Federal agencies to consider the environmental impact of their activities. Future development of the substantive rights and requirements imposed by the Act may be expected."[12] As a landmark in the evolving theory of public administration, the place of NEPA in history is being established, but its future as statutory law cannot be more than conjectured today. It is not possible to determine how the growing debate regarding the future of modern industrial society will be resolved.

For the near term, the effect of the Reagan presidency on environmental administration has yet to be ascertained. The

Reagan position appears to have been that the environmental protection measures of government have been carried to unnecessary lengths, burdening free enterprise and eroding personal liberties. But positions have changed in the course of presidencies, and the fate of NEPA under the Reagan administration cannot safely be predicted. As of early 1982 there has been little to suggest that it will be positive.[13]

The presently dominant position in American politics is that exponential economic and material growth may (must) continue indefinitely. Gross National Product takes precedence over environmental quality, although not over clearly established threats to health. But a minority view that society, in the interest of its own survival, should (must) phase into a so-called "steady or sustainable state" appears to be gaining support. Yet before the validity of either belief can be demonstrated, modern society may destroy itself through international or social war or through ecocatastrophe. In this debate NEPA is not overtly a commitment to either viewpoint. Its tendency has been to ameliorate the adverse side effects of growth. If the prescription of its Section 101 were followed, the direction of policy would almost necessarily be toward a stable or sustainable society.

Environment and Balanced Policy

Opponents and sometime friends of the environmental protection movement have regarded public interventions in the private sector on behalf of environmental quality as excessive. Although among some persons the name "environmentalist" has now become a bad word, almost no one declares himself as an enemy of environmental quality. Thus among the more plausible forms of indirect attack upon environmental policy and upon certain specific measures, such as restrictions on the use of pesticides or control of sulphur dioxide emissions, is a plea for balance. Efforts to return the environment to the status of a free enterprise commodity have often been couched in the language of moderation and a balancing of values, which in principle is hard to oppose but in practice often weighs heavily on the economic side of the scales.

For example, there is a National Council for Environmental Balance that appears to regard environmentalism as a conspiracy against American freedom and enterprise and undertakes to inform the American people of how the environmentalists plan autocratically to alter the American way of life. A different approach has been taken by John C. Whitaker in his book *Striking a Balance: Environment and Natural Resources Policy in the Nixon-Ford Years* (1976). This publication by the American Enterprise Institute for Public Policy Research takes a moderate and essentially honest view of the early implementation of the National Environmental Policy Act and complementary legislation. Nevertheless, this book and other writings and comments concerning the appropriate balance of environmental considerations in American public policy raise by implication some very fundamental questions regarding the relative importance of the environmental issue.

A number of writers holding similar views—A. Lawrence Chickering, Richard Neuhaus, and William Tucker, for instance—would persuade their readers that the environmental movement is a subterfuge for upper-middle-class selfishness.[14] A contrary conclusion has been reported by reliable opinion analysts, indicating substantial and growing support for environmental protection among all social classes even when posed as an alternative to economic growth. Nevertheless, the antienvironmentalist assertion that only a paper-thin minority of well-to-do elitists supports environmental quality measures continues to be repeated. But the *Congressional Quarterly*, after noting the removal of numbers of environmental advocates from positions in the federal government following the 1980 Reagan victory, concluded that although out, the environmentalists were not down, and that the environmental protection legislation of the preceding decade, having real public support, was not likely to be readily dismantled by the new administration.[15]

NEPA was enacted to achieve or restore a balance in American public policy that many persons believed had been lost in an overemphasis on economic, technological, and developmental values. In one of the leading interpretations of NEPA in the case of *Calvert Cliffs Coordinating Committee* v. *Atomic Energy Commission* (1972), Judge J. Skelly Wright described the balancing requirement of NEPA in the following words:

> NEPA mandates a case-by-case balancing judgment on the part of federal agencies.... The particular economic and technical benefit of planned action must be assessed and then weighed against the environmental cost: alternatives must be considered which would affect the balance of values.... In some cases the benefits will be great enough to justify a certain quantum of environmental costs; in other cases they will not be so great and the proposed action may have to be abandoned or significantly altered.... The point of the individualized balancing analysis is to insure that the optimally beneficial action is finally taken.[16]

In this language the court, in effect, prescribed a method but could not anticipate any particular response. Circumstances would influence decisions on cases. How are incommensurable values to be balanced and what values are appropriate in calculating costs and benefits? The theoretical test of balancing in a democratic political system is the extent to which the result corresponds to the preferred values of a society—to its prevalent norms. But how does one weigh differing values in a diverse, open, pluralistic society? Merely to argue for balance evades the issue, because balance is the issue over which adversaries on environmental policies differ.

In the striking of balances, the courts have relied upon legal procedures; public administrators have undertaken to use fiscal measures, chiefly through budgetary control. The use of fiscal and personnel controls to achieve a political regime's preferred balance among priorities and programs lies beyond our purview but not beyond our concern. However effective the striking of a balance may be for the purposes of the day, it may also reflect a deficiency of judgment concerning the relative importance of a range of issues to the welfare and survival of society. It may also indicate a laissez-faire premise that people will solve their own problems if government will just get out of their way. None of these premises provides the administrator with reliable criteria for making rational evaluation.

To the extent that people cannot agree upon the tests of truth, policy has no other basis than preponderance of political power. In the United States predominent political power has accepted evidence called "scientific" as capable of being tested for truth, that is, capable of possible disproof. But the extent to which the public generally believes scientific evidence to be more true than other forms of knowledge is not known. Public acceptance of scientific opinion appears to vary with the issue. Science appears most acceptable in policy areas in which no countervailing traditional, ideological, or religious opinion exists. Environmental issues often introduce unprecedented phenomena in events believed to be familiar. How NEPA fares in the 1980s will depend in large measure upon what people believe will be the consequences of present events as projected by science.

Regardless of pervading ideologies or social systems, society must ultimately confront the intransigency of nature. Bacon's dictum has not been refuted by the most sophisticated advances in science and technology. It may be true, as numerous commentators have declared, that environmental considerations are now well built into the fabric of American expectations and bureaucratic behavior. But I question whether the significance of this internalization of values and its implication for changes in behavior are adequately appreciated either by the people generally or by their political and administrative representatives and journalistic mentors. Three lines of evidence lead me to this conclusion.

The first is the continuing failure of the Congress or the executive branch to support extensive and long-term study of ecosystems dynamics and their social implications that sound long-range government policy requires. This failure seems to indicate a lack of appreciation on the part either of the public or of the government that the extent of our knowledge regarding the natural world and man's relationships to it is not adequate to ensure against the unwise and even disastrous misuse of our resource base. Even many prestigious members of the scientific community are not persuaded of real danger or of the necessity or feasibility of a major investment in a synthesizing environmental science.

Studies are now under way to discover the extent to which the basic requirements of NEPA for the use of scientific information and methodology (contained in subsections 102(2)(a), (b), and (h)) are taken seriously in agency planning and decisionmaking. In the mid-1970s, after examining five years of agency response to these requirements, a plausible verdict was that they had "not been strongly observed."[17] Major causal factors in this nonobservance were inadequacy in the content and format of scientific information and inadequacy of existing research methodology to investigate not only large and complex environmental problems but often small ones as well. The existing state of science continues to be inadequate to satisfy the policy goals of NEPA.

This anomaly was recognized by some of the drafters of the act, who saw in its requirements a means to enable society to discover things that it ought to know in a world increasingly exposed to the power of applied science and technology. Under Sections 204 and 205 of NEPA, the CEQ was given authority to take action toward this end. That it has never been permitted to take more than token action illustrates the almost congenital preference of politicians for symbol over substance. The initiative by CEQ member Gordon J. McDonald to establish the Nixon-endorsed environmental policy research institute with joint public-private funding was a positive gesture in the right direction.[18] But the abrupt cutoff of this effort, apparently in a show of political vindictiveness in the White House, suggests that high-level commitment to it was never strong. Yet there is a reason to agree with John C. Whitaker that "a great opportunity was missed."[19]

Congress has no doubt refused consistently to fund institutions designed specifically for comprehensive policy-oriented ecological research because it perceives no client for the product that it would regard as politically influential. In principle it has been possible to persuade the Congress that such inquiry is desirable, but in practice it will not appropriate the money needed to permit it to occur.

The NEPA requirement is only one among other cases in point. Under Title I, Section 122, of the River and Harbor Act of 1970 and Section 102 of the Omnibus Water Resource Act of 1970, the Congress required that social impacts be studied in addition to economic and environmental questions. The Corps of Engineers was given responsibility for undertaking these analyses but might have inferred that their presence in the statutes was largely symbolic because they were told that no additional money would be allocated to undertake the analyses. Nevertheless, the corps through its Institute of Water Resources Research has continued to seek ways to improve the method and content of social impact analysis. It has, for example, identified twelve types of analytic methods to ascertain social impacts. The infusion of social analysis knowledge and skills in the corps EIS process has been relatively slow, but it appears to be gaining acceptance and sophistication, helping managers "to understand their external environments, to cope with internal resource constraints and to manage uncertainty."[20]

Comprehensive research on energy policy found no constituency in official Washington before the Arab oil embargo of 1973. Insofar as government concern was manifest it was for the siting and planning of enlarged energy facilities or over the contentious issue of energy pricing. Since 1973 the supply side of energy research has been a "growth industry" although the fortunes of unconventional energy resources have varied with the ups and downs of public and congressional opinion regarding the prospect for the continued use of conventional fuels. The social implications of energy policy have been largely neglected in government-sponsored research.

The second line of evidence, suggesting that the environmental consciousness of Americans is an insufficient match to the vulnerability of their circumstances, lies in the failure of Congress to accept an environmental impact analysis as a restraint upon its own legislative procedures, including appropriations. Congressmen bridle at the thought of having their freedom to bargain and manipulate inhibited by unavoidable public disclosure of facts and evidence regarding choices of priorities and responsibility for public choices. It will be for the future to reveal whether the present democratic methods of the United States Congress are adequate to preserve the country from serious ecological consequences of business-as-usual priorities. It is possible that under *force majeure* Congress may consent to a reformation of its own procedures. At present, however, this possibility must be placed in the category of the more rarefied aspects of political conjecture. Congressmen represent constituents and clients among whose priorities environmental considerations are important but seldom the highest.

The final line of evidence is the astonishing fact that ten years after passage of the National Environmental Policy Act a major government agency and presidential administration could endorse so environmentally destructive a proposition as the land-based MX mobile system. It is a trenchant commentary on the state of environmental awareness and commitment in the government of the United States that, given the defense alternatives, such an ecological and economic monstrosity was seriously considered, and by the Carter administration, which ostensibly was concerned with environmental quality. It is equally preposterous that a government that declines to make an adequate investment in ecological research of the broad systems type that the goals of NEPA require would nevertheless seriously consider a proposal of such potentially environmentally destructive proportions that the expenditure of an estimated $17 million on an MX environmental impact statement was required. But it is encouraging that the mobile version of MX deployment aroused sufficient protest, especially in western states were environmentalism was alleged to be weak, that the strategy was abandoned. Economic and military reasons may have been decisive in the Reagan decision to abandon the mobile system, but environmental factors were also important—sufficiently so, perhaps, to sway the decision.

And so I cannot agree with optimists who believe that our environmental problems are under control. On the contrary, serious problems of accommodating human needs and desires in the world that nature has provided remain to be solved—many yet to be addressed and still others to be discovered. The most realistic assessment of our circumstances is that a beginning has been made and high goals have been set that, if conscientiously pursued, offer a chance that the future may prove brighter than present trends suggest.

NEPA and the Future

As of mid-1982, however, only an optimist could feel assurance that the goals articulated in NEPA would in the short run be conscientiously pursued. For the first time since enactment of the environmental statutes of the 1960s and 1970s, the federal government was controlled by persons who regarded this legislation as overreactive, elitist, and burdensome to the economy. As of the beginning of its second year in office, the extent to which or the speed with which the Reagan administration would move toward dismantling environmental protection and enhancement measures was uncertain. A substantial body of environmental law was in place that could not readily be repealed. Reliable surveys of public opinion continue to show widespread support for environmental quality measures considered in relation to costs and other policy priorities. Moreover, environmental values, most strongly held among the younger age groups of the population, might be expected *(caeteris paribus)* to gain additional strength politically with the passing of time.

Thus far, the environmental movement, cutting across most other lines of division in society, has been only moderately polarizing. Yet there are indications, as yet contrary to the major trend, that polarization on certain environmental issues might increase. As official or corporate intransigence confronts a growing militancy among more radical environmentalists, threats of violence become more frequent. Antinuclear protest has nurtured polarization and has become a rallying point for other and not necessarily related discontents. The term "ecotage" has been invented to describe the deliberate destruction of environmental values in historic sites, scenic areas, wildlife, or other objects of public protection so that there will be nothing to protect. This form of ecotage has chiefly been the work of private property owners indignant over public intrusion, or of land developers, corporate enterprisers, and laborers whose interests are threatened by efforts to prevent the use of particular lands or resources for economic purposes. Timber workers have threatened to use their chain saws to ruin redwood trees being taken out of production for preservation in a national park.

It should be added, however, that corporate enterprise has also contributed generously to environmental protection efforts, as for example in projects of The Nature Conservancy, and that individual landowners have often protected ecologically valuable sites at considerable economic sacrifice. A contrasting form of ecotage is damage to equipment or installations of engineering, mining, or utility firms used for purposes that the attackers perceive as environmentally destructive.

The pattern of reciprocal violence may not become established unless a national consensus for environmental policy fails to coalesce. It now appears that when NEPA was enacted there may have been less consensus than was widely assumed. In retrospect, it appears that there was a minority, then largely silent, that did not speak out against the pro-environment trend, but neither accepted its premises nor approved of its objectives.

With the apparent conservative trend that accompanied the Reagan presidential victory of 1980, this antienvironmentalist opposition from both left and right became more vocal and even gained fashionable acceptance. Slick paper magazines such as *Harpers* and *Atlantic,* whose editorial policies had previously appeared to lean toward environmentalism, featured articles questioning the authenticity of environmental concerns and portraying environmental protectionists as another self-interested pressure group (and one of the less meritorious, at that). The larger private philanthropic foundations generally appear to have lost interest in environmental issues, although some assist specific efforts in what may be an "exception" principle.

Journalistic cynicism toward the environmental movement does not, in my judgment, indicate a major shift of public opinion nor does it indicate a new or lasting trend. I think it more probable that the enthusiastic exposures of the "fraudulent" character of environmentalism are the "last hurrahs" of traditional attitudes that refuse to be displaced without protest. By analogy, throwing a brick through a shiny plate glass window makes a lot of noise and provides some notice for the brick-thrower. And the effort is much less than the painstaking effort of making and installing the window. Environmental protection is difficult and complex, and diligent search will almost certainly be rewarded by finding something to condemn or ridicule.

Contrary to the counterattack on environmentalism, the continuing consistency of the findings of opinion sampling in the United States and abroad strongly supports the conclusion that basic change has been occurring in the social-environmental paradigm of Western society. Discrepancies between the environmentally neutral to negative pronouncements of some leaders in politics, labor, and business and the contrary evidence of the polls may be partially explained by the factor of age. Persons past fifty years came to maturity before the advent of "the age of ecology." Environmental education was not a part of their experience. Although majorities in all age groups favor environmental protection, the margin is narrowest among persons over fifty. To the extent that a generation gap exists, it would appear to be one of timing and not of aging. With the passing of time, the indifferent or negative attitudes of the older minority will probably be replaced by the more environmentally concerned attitudes of presently younger people.

In large part, the rationale of the critics of environmentalism follows from extrapolation of the past into the future. Making selective use of statistics, they purport to demonstrate that environmental conditions have been getting better—that natural resources are becoming more abundant and that growing population means more creativity, more economic growth, and growing affirmation of man's mission to master the earth and colonize other worlds. Environmental protection, beyond essential minimals such as safeguarding drinking water and sequestering toxic wastes, is viewed as largely unnecessary.

It is evident that the environment issue (pro and con) has sometimes been used as a vehicle for advancing other causes. But there remains a substantial popular commitment to environmental protection apart from ideological biases. This has been the repeated finding of different and unrelated opinion polls over at least a decade. A *New York Times*/CBS poll published in the 4 October 1981 Sunday *New York Times* indicated that "although the degrees of intensity vary, support for strong environmental protection...cuts across age, income, education, and racial lines and even political parties and ideological groups. Republicans and Democrats, liberals and conservatives all indicated support for strong anti-pollution laws."

In projecting possible futures for environmental policy in America, examination of its trends elsewhere may have pertinence. The environmental debate in America has seldom taken account of the worldwide character of the growth of environmental awareness. Attitudinal studies by Lester Milbrath and others have revealed a European pattern of value change comparable to that found in America. Environmental concern among some Third World countries has developed to an extent that a decade ago would have seemed implausible. If American environmental politics is influenced by factors operating throughout the world, causal factors would appear to transcend exclusively American experience. Some scholars see in this development a new social paradigm or way of understanding the world that would be very consistent with NEPA goals and values.

Popular concern for environmental protection is not unique to the United States; evidence of it may be found in Canada, northwestern Europe, Australia, and New Zealand. Even in the Third World, governments and science elites have shown concern not yet shared by the general populations of their countries. The United Nations Environment Programme has stimulated Third World responsiveness to environmental concerns, and the World Bank has built environmental analysis into its preinvestment survey procedures. Among nongovernment organizations, the International Council of Scientific Unions, notably through the Scientific Committee on Problems of the Environment, as well as the International Union for Conservation of Nature and Natural Resources have assisted the development of environmental awareness and of competence in environmental monitoring and protection measures.

In these and many other organized efforts, the National Environmental Policy Act, and especially the administration of its environmental impact requirement, has been instructive and exemplary. The influence of NEPA in other countries has been periodically surveyed in the annual reports of the Council on Environmental Quality. Adaptation of NEPA principles rather than adoption of American procedures has been the more common occurrence. Concern for the environment is now demonstrably worldwide, but it must compete everywhere for attention and support with issues of greater political force and immediacy.

As of 1982, it seems probable that the new and growing commitment to environmental quality can, at best, do no more than slow the pace of general global environmental deterioration. To the extent that enclaves of protected environments are preserved in their natural states, genetic material may be kept available for the future restoration of impoverished and degraded ecosystems. The fact that NEPA was enacted and has worked to reorient public attitudes and behaviors offers some basis for hope, although the environmental impacts of present and prospective human populations seem certain to destroy or grievously impair much of what remains of the natural world. Should the goals and values epitomized by NEPA become internalized in the American ethos, the United States may manage the transition to a sustainable society with less pain than will many other nations. The presently dominant demographic-economic trends throughout much of the world do not appear to be indefinitely sustainable, and the longer they are pushed the more painful and costly will be their reversal—if indeed reversal is feasible.

It seems likely that science and science-based technology will continue to play an increasing role in public policy and administration. Preceding chapters in this volume have described historic aspects of the growing interrelationships of government and science, with a focus on the uses of science in relation to environmental policy. But consequences of equal and perhaps greater social impact may follow from advances in the technosciences of information management and communication based on electronics and the computer, along with new findings in the biomedical sciences, especially in research relating to genetics, geriatrics, and immunology.

Those advances in the sciences and in related technologies are often mutually reinforcing—sometimes in unforeseen ways. In relation to politics and human behavior generally they imply trade-offs among freedoms. But the new powers and opportunities derived from science demand discipline and informed restraint. To benefit from them mankind must learn how to live with new inventions and to control their use. This learning is essential because the evolutionary process that has enabled the human species to invent science and technology has not moved as efficiently to instill within it innate capacities for foresight and forbearance.

In this larger perspective, NEPA may be seen as a contrived, institutionalized answer to a people's recognition of its own deficiencies. Through the impact assessment process written into law we compel ourselves, as participants in self-government, to do what we know should be done in undertaking actions that may have consequences not immediately apparent. The EIS process institutionalizes patience, caution, and looking before leaping. Few if any among the critics of NEPA would act in their personal affairs in the manner that government decisionmakers formerly acted in relation to the environment.

Legislation such as NEPA has been accepted because we are environment-shaping animals, sufficiently intelligent to recognize that our survival requires self-discipline. In this perception of our need to supplement our inherent nature with social inventions designed to protect us against our susceptibility to error may lie our best hope.

Appendix
The National Environmental
Policy Act of 1969,
as amended*

An Act to establish a national policy for the environment, to provide for the establishment of a Council on Environmental Quality, and for other purposes.

Be it enacted by the Senate and House of Representatives of the United States of America in Congress assembled, That this Act may be cited as the "National Environmental Policy Act of 1969."

PURPOSE

SEC. 2. The purposes of this Act are: To declare a national policy which will encourage productive and enjoyable harmony between man and his environment; to promote efforts which will prevent or eliminate damage to the environment and biosphere and stimulate the health and welfare of man; to enrich the understanding of the ecological systems and natural resources important to the Nation; and to establish a Council on Environmental Quality.

TITLE I
DECLARATION OF NATIONAL ENVIRONMENTAL POLICY

SEC. 101. (a) The Congress, recognizing the profound impact of man's activity on the interrelations of all components of the natural environment, particularly the profound influences of population growth, high-density urbanization, industrial expansion, resource exploitation, and new and expanding technological advances and recognizing further the critical importance of restoring and maintaining environmental quality to the overall welfare and development of man,

---

*Pub. L. 91–190, 42 U.S.C. 4321–4347, January 1, 1970, as amended by Pub. L. 94–52, July 3, 1975, and Pub. L. 94–83, August 9, 1975.

declares that it is the continuing policy of the Federal Government, in cooperation with State and local governments, and other concerned public and private organizations, to use all practicable means and measures, including financial and technical assistance, in a manner calculated to foster and promote the general welfare, to create and maintain conditions under which man and nature can exist in productive harmony, and fulfill the social, economic, and other requirements of present and future generations of Americans.

(b) In order to carry out the policy set forth in this Act, it is the continuing responsibility of the Federal Government to use all practicable means, consistent with other essential considerations of national policy, to improve and coordinate Federal plans, functions, programs, and resources to the end that the Nation may —

(1) fulfill the responsibilities of each generation as trustee of the environment for succeeding generations;

(2) assure for all Americans safe, healthful, productive, and esthetically and culturally pleasing surroundings;

(3) attain the widest range of beneficial uses of the environment without degradation, risk to health or safety, or other undesirable and unintended consequences;

(4) preserve important historic, cultural, and natural aspects of our national heritage, and maintain, wherever possible, an environment which supports diversity, and variety of individual choice;

(5) achieve a balance between population and resource use which will permit high standards of living and a wide sharing of life's amenities; and

(6) enhance the quality of renewable resources and approach the maximum attainable recycling of depletable resources.

(c) The Congress recognizes that each person should enjoy a healthful environment and that each person has a responsibility to contribute to the preservation and enhancement of the environment.

SEC. 102. The Congress authorizes and directs that, to the fullest extent possible: (1) the policies, regulations, and public laws of the United States shall be interpreted and administered in accordance with the policies set forth in this Act, and (2) all agencies of the Federal Government shall—

(a) Utilize a systematic, interdisciplinary approach which will insure the integrated use of the natural and social sciences and the environmental design arts in planning and in decisionmaking which may have an impact on man's environment;

(b) Identify and develop methods and procedures, in consultation with the Council on Environmental Quality established by title II of this Act, which will insure that presently unquantified environmental amenities and values may be given appropriate consideration in decisionmaking along with economic and technical considerations;

(c) Include in every recommendation or report on proposals for legislation and other major Federal actions significantly affecting the quality of the human environment, a detailed statement by the responsible official on—

(i) The environmental impact of the proposed action,

(ii) Any adverse environmental effects which cannot be avoided should the proposal be implemented,

(iii) Alternatives to the proposed action,

(iv) The relationship between local short-term uses of man's environment and the maintenance and enhancement of long-term productivity, and

(v) Any irreversible and irretrievable commitments of resources which would be involved in the proposed action should it be implemented.

Prior to making any detailed statement, the responsible Federal official shall consult with and obtain the comments of any Federal agency which has jurisdiction by law or special expertise with respect to any environmental impact involved. Copies of such statement and the comments and views of the appropriate Federal, State, and local agencies, which are authorized to develop and enforce environmental standards, shall be made available to the President, the Council on Environmental Quality and to the public as provided by section 552 of title 5, United States Code, and shall accompany the proposal through the existing agency review processes;

(d) Any detailed statement required under subparagraph (c) after January 1, 1970, for any major Federal action funded under a program of grants to States shall not be deemed to be legally insufficient solely by reason of having been prepared by a State agency or official, if:

(i) the State agency or official has statewide jurisdiction and has the responsibility for such action,

(ii) the responsible Federal official furnishes guidance and participates in such preparation,

(iii) the responsible Federal official independently evaluates such statement prior to its approval and adoption, and

(iv) after January 1, 1976, the responsible Federal official provides early notification to, and solicits the views of, any other State or any Federal land management entity of any action or any alternative thereto which may have significant impacts upon such State or affected Federal land management entity and, if there is any disagreement on such impacts, prepares a written assessment of such impacts and views for incorporation into such detailed statement.

The procedures in this subparagraph shall not relieve the Federal official of his responsibilities for the scope, objectivity, and content of the entire statement or of any other responsibility under this Act; and further, this subparagraph does not affect the legal sufficiency of statements prepared by State agencies with less than statewide jurisdiction.

(e) Study, develop, and describe appropriate alternatives to recommended courses of action in any proposal which involves unresolved conflicts concerning alternative uses of available resources;

(f) Recognize the worldwide and long-range character of environmental problems and, where consistent with the foreign policy of the United States, lend appropriate support to initiatives, resolutions, and programs designed to maximize international cooperation in anticipating and preventing a decline in the quality of mankind's world environment;

(g) Make available to States, counties, municipalities, institutions, and individuals, advice and information useful in restoring, maintaining, and enhancing the quality of the environment;

(h) Initiate and utilize ecological information in the planning and development of resource-oriented projects; and

(i) Assist the Council on Environmental Quality established by title II of this Act.

SEC. 103. All agencies of the Federal Government shall review their present statutory authority, administrative regulations, and current policies and procedures for the purpose of determining whether there are any deficiencies or inconsistencies therein which prohibit full compliance with the purposes and provisions of this Act and shall propose to the President not later than July 1, 1971, such measures as may be necessary to bring their authority and policies into conformity with the intent, purposes, and procedures set forth in this Act.

SEC. 104. Nothing in section 102 or 103 shall in any way affect the specific statutory obligations of any Federal agency (1) to comply with criteria or standards of environmental quality, (2) to coordinate or consult with any other Federal or State agency, or (3) to act, or refrain from acting contingent upon the recommendations or certification of any other Federal or State agency.

SEC. 105. The policies and goals set forth in this Act are supplementary to those set forth in existing authorizations of Federal agencies.

TITLE II
COUNCIL ON ENVIRONMENTAL QUALITY

SEC. 201. The President shall transmit to the Congress annually beginning July 1, 1970, an Environmental Quality Report (hereinafter referred to as the "report") which shall set forth (1) the status and condition of the major natural, manmade, or altered environmental classes of the Nation, including, but not limited to, the air, the aquatic, including marine, estuarine, and fresh water, and the terrestrial environment, including, but not limited to, the forest, dryland, wetland, range, urban, suburban and rural environment; (2) current and foreseeable trends in the quality, management and utilization of such environments and the effects of those trends on the social, economic, and other requirements of the Nation; (3) the adequacy of available natural resources for fulfilling human and economic requirements of the Nation in the light of expected population pressures; (4) a review of the programs and activities (including regulatory activities) of the Federal Government, the State and local governments, and nongovernmental entities or individuals with particular reference to their effect on the environment and on the conservation, development and utilization of natural resources; and (5) a program for remedying the deficiencies of existing programs and activities, together with recommendations for legislation.

SEC. 202. There is created in the Executive Office of the President a Council on Environmental Quality (hereinafter referred to as the "Council"). The Council shall be composed of three members who shall be appointed by the President to serve at his pleasure, by and with the advice and consent of the Senate. The President shall designate one of the members of the Council to serve as Chairman. Each member shall be a person who, as a result of his training, experience, and attainments, is exceptionally well qualified to analyze and interpret environmental trends and information of all kinds; to appraise programs and activities of the Federal Government in the light of the policy set forth in title I of this Act; to be conscious of and responsive to the scientific, economic, social, esthetic, and cultural needs and interests of the Nation; and to formulate and recommend national policies to promote the improvement of the quality of the environment.

SEC. 203. The Council may employ such officers and employees as may be necessary to carry out its functions under this Act. In addition, the Council may employ and fix the compensation of such experts and consultants as may be necessary for the carrying out of its functions under this Act, in accordance with section 3109 of title 5, United States Code (but without regard to the last sentence thereof).

SEC. 204. It shall be the duty and function of the Council—

(1) to assist and advise the President in the preparation of the Environmental Quality Report required by section 201 of this title;

(2) to gather timely and authoritative information concerning the conditions and trends in the quality of the environment both current and prospective, to analyze and interpret such information for the purpose of determining whether such conditions and trends are interfering, or are likely to interfere, with the achievement of the policy set forth in title I of this Act, and to compile and submit to the President studies relating to such conditions and trends;

(3) to review and appraise the various programs and activities of the Federal Government in the light of the policy set forth in title I of this Act for the purpose of determining the extent to which such programs and activities are contributing to the achievement of such policy, and to make recommendations to the President with respect thereto;

(4) to develop and recommend to the President national policies to foster and promote the improvement of environmental quality to meet the conservation, social, economic, health, and other requirements and goals of the Nation;

(5) to conduct investigations, studies, surveys, research, and analyses relating to ecological systems and environmental quality;

(6) to document and define changes in the natural environment, including the plant and animal systems, and to accumulate necessary data and other information for a continuing analysis of these changes or trends and an interpretation of their underlying causes;

(7) to report at least once each year to the President on the state and condition of the environment; and

(8) to make and furnish such studies, reports thereon, and recommendations with respect to matters of policy and legislation as the President may request.

SEC. 205. In exercising its powers, functions, and duties under this Act, the Council shall—

(1) Consult with the Citizens' Advisory Committee on Environmental Quality established by Executive Order No. 11472, dated May 29, 1969, and with such representatives of science, industry, agriculture, labor, conservation organizations, State and local governments and other groups, as it deems advisable; and

(2) Utilize, to the fullest extent possible, the services, facilities and information (including statistical information) of public and pri-

vate agencies and organizations, and individuals, in order that duplication of effort and expense may be avoided, thus assuring that the Council's activities will not unnecessarily overlap or conflict with similar activities authorized by law and performed by established agencies.

SEC. 206. Members of the Council shall serve full time and the Chairman of the Council shall be compensated at the rate provided for Level II of the Executive Schedule Pay Rates (5 U.S.C. 5313). The other members of the Council shall be compensated at the rate provided for Level IV of the Executive Schedule Pay Rates (5 U.S.C. 5315).

SEC. 207. The Council may accept reimbursements from any private nonprofit organization or from any department, agency, or instrumentality of the Federal Government, any State, or local government, for the reasonable travel expenses incurred by an officer or employee of the Council in connection with his attendance at any conference, seminar, or similar meeting conducted for the benefit of the Council.

SEC. 208. The Council may make expenditures in support of its international activities, including expenditures for: (1) international travel; (2) activities in implementation of international agreements; and (3) the support of international exchange programs in the United States and in foreign countries.

SEC. 209. There are authorized to be appropriated to carry out the provisions of this chapter not to exceed $300,000 for fiscal year 1970, $700,000 for fiscal year 1971, and $1,000,000 for each fiscal year thereafter.

Notes

Chapter 1

1. Personal communication.

2. *Man of the Environment,* National Institute of Mental Health, Unit for Research on Behavioral Systems, Doc. No. 161, 21 May 1970, pp. 3–4.

3. *City of New York* v. *United States,* 337 F.Supp. 150, 159, 20276 (E.D.N.Y. 1972).

4. Sally K. Fairfax, "A Disaster in the Environmental Movement," *Science* 199 (17 February 1978):747. For rejoinders to this curious article readers are referred to Letters to the Editor, *Science* 202 (8 December 1978). For a more general review of the criticisms of NEPA see Lynton K. Caldwell, "Is NEPA Inherently Self-Defeating?" *Environmental Law Reporter* 9 (January 1979):50001–07.

5. Malcolm F. Baldwin, *The Southwest Energy Complex: A Policy Evaluation* (Washington, D.C.: The Conservation Foundation, 1973).

6. U.S., Congress, Senate, Committee on Interior and Insular Affairs, *National Environment Policy: Hearing on S. 1075, S. 237, and S. 1752,* 91st Cong., 1st sess., 16 April 1979.

7. Ibid., p. 117.

8. Ibid.

9. Ibid., p. 116.

10. Bruce A. Ackerman and William T. Hassler, *Clean Coal–Dirty Air* (New Haven:Yale University Press, 1981), pp. 122–23.

11. The *Regulations* were first published in the *Federal Register* 43, No. 230 (29 November 1978):55978–56007 and have been reprinted

annually in *Environmental Quality,* the annual report of the Council on Environmental Quality.

12. This observation is corroborated in an article by Carol Komissaroff, "Environmental Law—The National Environmental Policy Act—Andrus v. Sierra Club," *New York Law School Review* 26 (1981):401. Reviewing the opinions of the Supreme Court in a number of NEPA litigations, and specifically with respect to *Andrus* v. *Sierra Club,* 442 U.S. 347 (1979), Komissaroff concludes that "there are several disturbing elements about the decision, not the least of which is the Supreme Court's reticence to strongly support NEPA policies. *Andrus* is the sixth NEPA case to come before the Court. On [the previous] five of the six occasions, the Court has very strictly construed the language of the Act in favor of the agencies. Given each of these opportunities to apply the *policies* of NEPA to agency avoidance of NEPA mandate, the Court has chosen instead to construe only the bare *words* of the Act."

13. Fairfax, "Disaster."

14. D. W. Shindler, "The Impact Statement Boondoggle," *Science* 192 (7 March 1976):509.

15. Ackerman and Hassler, *Clean Coal–Dirty Air,* p. 122.

16. On the applicability of NEPA abroad see the following: U.S. Department of Justice, "Assessment of Extraterritorial Environmental Impacts under NEPA and Executive Order 12114," *Land and Natural Resources Division Journal* 17 (September–October 1980):2–12; Dick Kirschten, "Exporting the Environment," *National Journal* 10 (25 February 1978):318; Francis M. Allegra, "Executive Order 12114—Environmental Effects Abroad: Does It Really Further the Purpose of NEPA?" *Cleveland State Law Review* 1 (1980):109–39; and Richard Carpenter and William Matthews, "NEPA: Environmental Innocence Abroad," *East-West Perspectives* 1 (Fall 1980):6–9.

17. See, for example, Samuel P. Hays, *Conservation and the Gospel of Efficiency: The Progressive Conservative Movement, 1890–1920* (Cambridge, Mass.: Harvard University Press, 1959); Frank E. Smith, *The Politics of Conservation* (New York: Pantheon Books, 1966); and Roderick Nash, ed., *The American Environment: Readings in the History of Conservation* (Reading, Mass.: Addison-Wesley, 1968).

Chapter 2

1. On the "officialization" of science see James E. King, *Science and Rationalism in the Government of Louis XIV* (Baltimore: Johns

Hopkins Press, 1949); Roger Hahn, *The Anatomy of a Scientific Institution: The Paris Academy of Sciences, 1666–1803* (Berkeley and Los Angeles: University of California Press, 1971); and Albion W. Small, *The Cameralists: Pioneers of Social Polity* (Chicago: University of Chicago Press, 1909).

2. But L. Pearce Williams concluded that Napoleonic patronage of the Ecole debased its scientific quality in the interest of military technology: "Science, Education and Napoleon I," *Isis* 47 (December 1956):369–82. Note also Robert Gilpin, "The Heritage of the Napoleonic System," Chapter 4 of *France in the Age of the Scientific State* (Princeton: Princeton University Press, 1968).

3. On the application of statistical analysis to national policies see John Koren, *The History of Statistics* (New York: Macmillan, 1918), and V. John, *Geschichte der Statistik* (Stuttgart: Enke, 1884, reprinted Wiesbaden: Saendig, 1968).

4. On reductionism as a scientific concept see Ernest Nagel, "The Meaning of Reductionism in the Natural Sciences," in Robert C. Stauffer, ed., *Science and Civilization* (Madison: University of Wisconsin Press, 1949), pp. 99–135.

5. A. Hunter Dupree, *Science in the Federal Government: A History of Policies and Activities to 1940* (Cambridge, Mass.: Harvard University Press, 1957); and Silvio A. Bedini, *Thinkers and Tinkers: Early American Men of Science* (New York: Charles Scribner's Sons, 1975). The four volumes of the studies in administrative history of the United States by Leonard D. White (New York: Macmillan, 1948–58) contain various accounts of the interplay of science and administrative policy.

6. For developments in this period see Samuel P. Hays, *Conservation and the Gospel of Efficiency: The Progressive Conservation Movement, 1890–1920* (Cambridge, Mass.: Harvard University Press, 1959).

7. See Lester W. Milbrath, "Environmental Values and Beliefs of the General Public and Leaders in the United States, England and Germany," in Dean Mann, ed., *Environmental Policy Formation: The Impact of Values, Ideology and Standards* (Lexington, Mass.: Lexington Books, 1981); and Lester W. Milbrath, *General Report: U.S. Component of a Comparative Study of Environmental Beliefs and Values* (Buffalo, N.Y.: State University of New York at Buffalo, Environmental Studies Center, January 1981). See also U.S. Department of Agriculture, U.S. Department of Energy, and Environmental Protection Agency, *Public Opinion on Environmental Issues: Results of a National Public Opinion Survey* (Washington, D.C.: U.S. Government Printing Office, 1981); abstract in *Environmental Quality–1980: Eleventh Annual Report of the Council on Environmental Quality,* December 1980, Appendix A.

8. Vannevar Bush, *Science, the Endless Frontier: A Report to the President on a Program for Postwar Scientific Research* (Washington, D.C.: U.S. Office of Scientific Research and Development, July 1945). For the role of scientists in the controversies over public policy during this period see Robert Gilpin and Christopher Wright, eds., *Scientists and National Policymaking* (New York: Columbia University Press, 1969).

9. *Public Papers of the Presidents of the United States: Richard Nixon, 1971* (Washington, D.C.: U.S. Government Printing Office, 1971), p. 4.

10. *Environmental Defense Fund* v. *Corps of Engineers,* 470 F.2d 289, 2ELR20740 (8th Cir. 1971), and *Calvert Cliffs Coordinating Committee* v. *Atomic Energy Commission,* 449 F.2d 1109, 1ELR20346 (D.C. Cir. 1971).

11. John M. Gaus and Leon O. Wolcott, *Public Administration and the United States Department of Agriculture* (Chicago: Public Administration Service, 1940); see especially Chapter 7, "Production." See also Leonard D. White, "The Department of Agriculture," in *The Republicans, 1869–1901: A Study in Administrative History* (New York: Macmillan, 1958), pp. 232–56.

12. By J. E. S. Fawcett in *Outer Space and International Order,* Annual Memorial Lecture (London: David Davies Memorial Institute of International Studies, 1964), p. 3.

13. Albert Schweitzer, *Out of My Life and Thought: An Autobiography,* trans. C. T. Campion (New York: Holt, Rinehart and Winston, 1949), p. 241.

Chapter 3

1. U.S., Congress, Senate Committee on Interior and Insular Affairs and House Committee on Science and Astronautics, *Joint House-Senate Colloquium to Discuss a National Policy for the Environment: Hearings,* 90th Cong., 2d sess., 17 July 1968.

2. U.S., Congress, Senate, *Congressional Record,* 89th Cong., 1st sess., 13 July 1965, pp. 16616, 16619–20; and U.S., Congress, Senate, Committee on Interior and Insular Affairs, *Ecological Research and Surveys: Hearing on S. 2282,* 89th Cong., 2d sess., 27 April 1966.

3. *Calvert Cliffs Coordinating Committee* v. *Atomic Energy Commis-*

sion, 449 F.2d 1109, 1114; 1 ELR20346, 20348 (1971).

4. Peter W. House, *The Quest for Completeness: Comprehensive Analysis in Environmental Management and Planning* (Lexington, Mass.: Lexington Books, 1976), p. xxxvi.

5. John C. Whitaker, *Striking a Balance: Environment and Natural Resource Policy in the Nixon-Ford Years* (Washington, D.C.: American Enterprise Institute for Public Policy Research, 1976), p. 52. An alternative explanation of the waning influence of the CEQ after 1972 was the increasing preoccupation of the Nixon White House with Vietnam and Watergate and the inability of President Ford to conceptualize the environmental issue. During the more environment-conscious Carter administration the influence of the CEQ notably revived.

6. Max Nicholson, *The Environmental Revolution: A Guide for the New Masters of the Earth* (New York: McGraw-Hill, 1970).

7. House, *Quest for Completeness,* p. xxxvi.

8. Daniel A. Mazmanian and Jeanne Nienaber, *Can Organizations Change? Environmental Protection, Citizen Participation, and the Corps of Engineers* (Washington, D.C.: Brookings Institution, 1979).

9. For further discussion of the grazing permits issue see Paul J. Culhane, *Public Land Politics: Interest Group Influence on the Forest Service and the Bureau of Land Management* (Baltimore: The Johns Hopkins University Press for Resources for the Future, 1981). A critical but incomplete account of the issue was reported by Eugene Bardach and Lucian Pugliaresi in "The Environmental Impact Statement vs. the Real World," *Public Interest* 49 (Fall 1977):22–39.

10. Comment, "The National Environmental Policy Act: How It Is Working, How It Should Work," *Environmental Law Reporter* 4 (1974):10003.

Chapter 4

1. "The National Environmental Policy Act: Status and Accomplishments," *Transactions of the Thirty-Eighth North American Wildlife and Natural Resources Conference, March 18–21, 1973* (Washington, D.C.: Wildlife Management Institute, 1973), pp. 19–30.

2. *Calvert Cliffs Coordinating Committee v. Atomic Energy Commission,* 449 F.2d 1109, 1115, 1ELR20346, 20349 (1971).

3. William H. Rodgers, Jr., *Handbook on Environmental Law* (St. Paul, Minn.: West Publishing Co., 1977), pp. 719–20.

4. See Henry C. Hart, "Governing the Missouri," *Iowa Law Review* 41 (Winter 1956):198–215, and *The Dark Missouri* (Madison: University of Wisconsin Press, 1957); and Marian E. Ridgeway, *The Missouri Basin's Pick-Sloan Plan: A Case Study in Congressional Policy Determination,* Illinois Studies in the Social Sciences, No. 35 (Urbana: University of Illinois Press, 1955).

5. Information on the California Desert Plan is based on interviews with resource specialist Kristin H. Berry (1 March 1981), with managers of the BLM California Desert District (16 September 1981), and with Robert Jones of the BLM Office of Planning, Inventory, and Environmental Coordination (5 November 1981).

6. Christopher K. Leman, "The Forest Ranger Revisited: Administrative Behavior in the U.S. Forest Service in the 1980s," paper presented at the 1981 Annual Meeting of the American Political Science Association, New York City, 3–6 September 1981, and citing Thomas C. Nelson, "The Evolution of National Forest Planning," *Forest Planning* 1 (April 1980):13–14.

7. Nancy J. Doemel, *The Garrison Diversion Unit: Science, Technology, Politics, and Values* (Bloomington:Indiana University, Advanced Studies in Science, Technology, and Public Policy, 1979).

8. See Council on Environmental Quality, *Environmental Impact Statements–An Analysis of Six Years' Experience by Seventy Federal Agencies* (Washington, D.C.: Council on Environmental Quality, 1976).

9. Note the observation of Roger Cramton, former chairman of the Administrative Conference of the United States, that under NEPA, "an agency that attempts to grapple meaningfully with environmental issues is forced to recruit a phalanx of professionals with different values and perspectives than its old-line operatives," cited by Robert Gillette, "The Power of NEPA," in Ann Gilliam, ed., *Voices for the Earth* (San Francisco: Science Club Books, 1979), p. 465. For a more complete statement of Cramton's observations, see "On Leading a Horse to Water: NEPA and the Federal Bureaucracy," *Michigan Law Review* 71 (January 1973):511–36.

10. David Atlas, ed., *Atmospheric Science and Public Policy* (Boston: American Meteorological Society, 1976), pp. 31, 76.

11. *Lathan* v. *Brinegar* (11), 506 F.2d 677–93; ELR4, 20802, 2808 (9th Cir. 1974), quoting *McNabb* v. *United States,* 318 U.S. 332, 347, 635.

12. J. Skelly Wright, "New Judicial Requisites for Informal Rulemaking: Implications for the Environmental Impact Statement Process," *Administrative Law Review* 29 (Winter 1977):59, 60, 64.

Chapter 5

1. For a historical account of the shifting emphases in American science in relation to social policy see Ronald C. Tobey, *The American Ideology of National Science, 1919–1930* (Pittsburgh: University of Pittsburgh Press, 1971).

2. Gary W. Barrett, "Environmental Impact Assessment—An Introduction," *Ohio Journal of Science* 78 (July 1978):204–05.

3. See J. E. De Steiguer and R. G. Merryfield, "The Impact of the Environmental Era on Forestry Education in North America," *Unasylva* 31, no. 123 (1979):21–25.

4. *Environmental Education: Academia's Response* (Washington, D.C.: American Institute of Biological Sciences, 1972).

5. "Letters," *Harpers,* July 1981, p. 6.

6. S. 3410 (6 February 1970 Baker); S. 1216 (12 March 1971 Jackson); for an account of the National Environmental Laboratory proposal see David J. Rose, "New Laboratories for Old," *Daedalus* 102 (Summer 1974):145–55.

7. C. S. Holling, ed., *Adaptive Environmental Assessment and Management* (New York: John Wiley, 1978). For an example of IIASA analytic studies see *IIASA Reports,* a quarterly journal published beginning in 1980.

8. Interview, 27 March 1981, Denver, Colorado.

9. Interview, 8 May 1981, Baltimore, Maryland.

10. E.g., investigations by Serge Taylor at Stanford University and a group at Indiana University working under my direction.

Chapter 6

1. The debate is not unique to the United States. There is a European literature, and for Canada see F. Ronald Hayes, *The Chaining of Prometheus: Evolution of a Power Structure for Canadian Science* (Toronto: University of Toronto Press, 1973).

2. These controversies have been well summarized by Mary E. Ames in *Outcome Uncertain: Science and the Political Process* (Washington, D.C.: Communications Press, 1978).

3. U.S., Congress, House, *Report of the Subcommittee on Science, Research, and Development to the Committee on Science and Astronautics,* 89th Cong., 2d sess., 1968, pp. 3–8.

4. Richard Carpenter, "The Scientific Basis of NEPA—Is It Adequate?" *Environmental Law Reporter* 6 (1976):50014. See also Herbert C. Morton, "The Environmental Data Dilemma," *Resources,* No. 66 (Spring 1981), pp. 22–23.

5. James C. Hite, *Room and Situation: The Political Economy of Land-Use Policy* (Chicago: Nelson-Hall, 1979), p. 196.

6. Council on Environmental Quality and Department of State, *The Global 2000 Report to the President: Entering the Twenty-first Century,* 3 vols. (Washington, D.C.: Council on Environmental Quality, 1980).

7. U.S., Congress, House, Subcommittee on Fisheries and Wildlife Conservation of the Committee on Merchant Marine and Fisheries, *Hearings on H.R. 17436, H.R. 17779, H.R. 18141,* 91st Cong., 2d sess., 2, 3, 25, and 26 June 1970. But the data problem continues unresolved. See Morton, "Environmental Data Dilemma."

8. Interview, 7 May 1981, Washington, D.C.

9. Interview, 26 March 1981, Cheyenne, Wyoming.

10. Granville H. Sewell and Susan Kerrick, "The Fate of EIS Projects: A Retrospective Study," paper presented at a National Symposium at The Institute of Man and Science, Rensselaerville, N.Y., 18–23 May 1980.

11. Granville H. Sewell, *Final Report to the National Science Foundation Division of Policy Research and Analysis on the Quality of Scientific Considerations Affecting the Environment* (New York: Columbia University, School of Public Health, Faculty of Medicine, Division of Health Sciences, June 1981). For an analysis of the scientific quality of EISs focused upon one particular issue see Paul J. Culhane, Thomas V. Armentano, and H. Paul Friesema, *State-of-the-Art Scientific Understanding of Acid Deposition in Environmental Assessments on Fossil-Fuel Powerplants* (Indianapolis: Institute of Ecology, August 1981).

12. Arnold W. Reitze, *Environmental Law,* 2d ed. (Washington, D.C.: North American International, 1972), Chapter 1, p. 50.

13. But see Andy Pasztor, "White House Seen Moving to Soften Stance on Environmental Issues," *Wall Street Journal* (23 April 1982):6.

14. For example, A. Lawrence Chickering, "Taking James Watt off the Hook," *Newsweek* (1 June 1981):10; Richard J. Neuhaus, *In Defense of People* (1971); and William Tucher, "Environmentalism and the Leisure Class," *Harper's Magazine* (December 1977):49–.

15. *Congressional Quarterly: Weekly Report* 39 (31 January 1981):211–16. See also the citations to surveys in Chapter 2, note 7. In addition, note especially testimony by pollster Louis Harris before the

House of Representatives Subcommittee on Health and Environment of the Committee on Energy and Commerce, 15 October 1981.

16. 449 F.2d at 1123, 1 ELR at 20353.

17. William H. Rodgers, Jr., *Handbook on Environmental Law* (St. Paul, Minn.: West Publishing Co., 1977), p. 723.

18. See *Public Papers of the Presidents of the United States: Richard Nixon, 1970* (Washington, D.C.: U.S. Government Printing Office, 1971), "Special Message to Congress Proposing the 1971 Environmental Program," 8 February, p. 141.

19. John C. Whitaker, *Striking a Balance: Environment and Natural Resource Policy in the Nixon-Ford Years* (Washington, D.C.: American Enterprise Institute for Public Policy Research, 1976), p. 333.

20. Jerry Delli Priscoli, "People and Water: Social Impact Assessment Research," *Water Spectrum* 13 (Summer 1981):11.

Bibliographical Note

The National Environmental Policy Act has generated a large literature, much of which relates only in part to the focus of this book. The
greater part of these writings are concerned with the environmental
impact statement. This book, concerned with the uses of science in
NEPA in relation to the policy it declares, deals with the EIS primarily
as a means through which science in its several meanings has been
used to redirect policy through procedural reform.

A voluminous body of literature has been published on the methodology of environmental impact analysis, ranging from cookbook-
type manuals to the solid and often-cited *Adaptive Environmental
Assessment and Management,* edited by C. S. Holling (New York: John
Wiley, 1978).

The plurality of writings on NEPA and the EIS appears in law
reviews, casebooks, and legal reports. Rulings and litigation involving
NEPA are reported, among other places, in the *Environmental Law
Reporter* (Environmental Law Institute, 1971–) and the *Environment
Reporter* (Bureau of National Affairs, 1970–). Following are leading
casebooks on environmental law in which NEPA receives thorough
coverage: Erica L. Dolgin and Thomas G. P. Guilbert, eds., *Federal
Environmental Law* (St. Paul, Minn.: West Publishing Co., 1974);
Frank Grad, *Treatise on Environmental Law* (New York: Matthew
Bender, 1978); Oscar S. Gray, *Cases and Materials on Environmental
Law* (Washington, D.C.: Bureau of National Affairs, 1971); Eva Hanks,
A. Dan Tarlock, and John Hanks, *Environmental Law and Policy* (St.
Paul, Minn.: West Publishing Co., 1974); James E. Krier, *Environmen-
tal Law and Policy* (Indianapolis: Bobbs-Merrill, 1971); Norman J.
Landau and Paul D. Rheingold, *The Environmental Law Handbook*
(New York: Ballantine Books, 1971); Charles J. Meyers and A. Dan

Tarlock, *Selected Legal and Economic Aspects of Environmental Protection* (Mineola, N.Y.: Foundation Press, 1971); Neil Orloff and George Brooks, *The National Environmental Policy Act: Cases and Materials* (Washington, D.C.: Bureau of National Affairs, 1980); Arnold W. Reitze, Jr., *Environmental Law, Volume I,* 2d ed. (Washington, D.C.: North American International, 1972); William H. Rodgers, Jr., *Handbook on Environmental Law* (St. Paul, Minn.: West Publishing Co., 1977); and Edwin Wallace Tucker, *Text, Cases, Problems on Legal Regulation of the Environment* (St. Paul, Minn.: West Publishing Co., 1972).

In addition to the present volume, three books have been written dealing with NEPA as a whole: Frederick Anderson, *NEPA in the Courts: A Legal Analysis of the National Environmental Policy Act* (Baltimore: The Johns Hopkins University Press, 1973); Richard N. L. Andrews, *Environmental Policy and Administrative Change* (Lexington, Mass.: Lexington Books, 1976); and Richard A. Liroff, *A National Policy for the Environment: NEPA and Its Aftermath* (Bloomington: Indiana University Press, 1976). Unfortunately for the contemporary reader, all three books deal with NEPA as it was administered and interpreted during its first half decade and do not assess cumulative experience with the act after formulation of the regulations by the CEQ late in 1978. Nevertheless, these books continue to provide benchmarks for the progressive development of policy, adjudication, and administration under the act.

The most complete and comprehensive legislative history of NEPA is a doctoral dissertation by Terence T. Finn, "Conflict and Compromise: Congress Makes a Law—The Passage of the National Environmental Policy Act" (Georgetown University, December 1972). Probably the two most important official documents relating to the purpose are: U.S., Congress, Senate Committee on Interior and Insular Affairs and House Committee on Science and Astronautics, *Joint House-Senate Colloquium to Discuss a National Policy for the Environment: Hearings,* 90th Cong., 2d sess., 17 July 1968, No. 8, pp. 87–127, also reprinted in U.S., Congress, Senate, *Congressional Record,* 91st Cong., 1st sess., 18 February 1969, 115, pt. 3:3701–08; and U.S., Congress, Senate, Committee on Interior and Insular Affairs, *National Environmental Policy: Hearing on S. 1075, S. 237, and S. 1752,* 91st Cong., 1st sess. 16 April 1969, pp. 128–35.

Beginning in December 1975, a series of official reviews and evaluations of experience with NEPA have been undertaken. Principal among these are: U.S., Congress, House, Subcommittee on Fisheries

and Wildlife Conservation and the Environment of the Committee on
Merchant Marine and Fisheries, *Workshop on the National Environmental Policy Act,* 94th Cong., 2d sess., Committee Print, 1976; U.S.,
Congress, House, Subcommittee on Fisheries and Wildlife Conservation and the Environment of the Committee on Merchant Marine and
Fisheries, *Administration of the National Environmental Policy Act,*
91st Cong., 2d sess., Committee Print, 1970, Parts 1–2 and Appendix;
U.S., Congress, House, Subcommittee on Fisheries and Wildlife Con-
servation and the Environment of the Committee on Merchant Marine
and Fisheries, *Administration of the National Environmental Policy
Act–1972,* 92d Cong., 2d sess., Committee Print, 1972; and U.S., Congress, House, Subcommittee on Fisheries and Wildlife Conservation
and the Environment of the Committee on Merchant Marine and
Fisheries, *Oversight Hearings on the Administration of the National
Environmental Policy Act of 1969,* 94th Cong., 2d sess., Committee
Print, 1976; General Accounting Office, *Improvements Needed in
Federal Efforts to Implement the National Environmental Policy Act of
1969* (B170186, 18 May 1972); General Accounting Office, *The En-
vironmental Impact Statement—It Seldom Causes Long Project Delays
But Could Be More Useful If Prepared Earlier* (CED 77-99, 9 August
1977); General Accounting Office, *The Council on Environmental Qual-
ity: A Tool in Shaping National Policy* (CED-81-66, 19 March 1981);
*Environmental Impact Statements: A Report of the Commission on
Federal Paper Work* (25 February 1977); and Council on Environmental Quality, *Environmental Impact Statements—An Analysis of Six
Years' Experience by Seventy Federal Agencies* (Washington, D.C.:
Council on Environmental Quality, 1976).

For writings on NEPA since 1976, Richard A. Liroff has provided a
comprehensive listing as a note to his article "NEPA—Where Have We
Been and Where Are We Going?" in the *APA Journal* (April 1980). To
my knowledge no one has undertaken a critical review of this literature, analyzing not only the writers' opinions but the basis for their
views as evidenced in their sources of data, corroborative support, and
the nature and extent of personal experience. Such analysis would be
useful to readers who are unable to determine what weight to accord
various judgments regarding NEPA. This should not be an exercise
primarily to determine who is right and who is wrong in evaluations of
NEPA, although not all conclusions are likely to be equally right. Its
purpose would be to ascertain the opinions of a self-selected group of
NEPA scholars regarding the efficacy of the act. There would be a
range of opinion, and it could be instructive to compare opinions,
particularly at the extremes, with their supporting data or evidence.

My own involvement in the genesis of NEPA as consultant to the Senate Committee on Interior and Insular Affairs during its drafting could lead to the opinion that I have been uncritically committed to the act. I will concede my commitment to NEPA, but not to being uncritical. I have criticized certain distortions and misapplications of NEPA in "The Environmental Impact Statement: A Misused Tool," Ravinder K. Jain and Bruce L. Hutchings, eds., *Environmental Impact Analysis: Emerging Issues in Planning,* (Urbana: University of Illinois Press, 1978). But I have also addressed criticisms of NEPA that in my judgment ignored substantial evidence that would have pointed toward different conclusions. In my article "Is NEPA Inherently Self-Defeating?" *(Environmental Law Reporter* 9 [January 1979]:50001–07), I examined some of the more frequent allegations regarding NEPA's effectiveness and their basis in actual experience. As I have read the evidence, attacks upon NEPA as counterproductive have in no case been based on the substantial evidence available concerning administration of the act. Most appear to reflect selected "worst cases," subjective impression, and hearsay.

As this book went to press, several studies of the administration of NEPA were nearing completion. These included our study of ways to improve the scientific content and methodology of environmental impact analysis (NSF Grant No. PRA 79-10014) and an analysis by the CEQ of comments received regarding regulations issued under Executive Order 11991, 24 May 1977. Recently available was a study by the Environmental Law Institute, *NEPA in Action: Environmental Offices in Nineteen Federal Agencies* (Washington, D.C., 1981).

To assess the effectiveness of NEPA fairly, its record must be compared with that of other legislation, particularly with novel and policy-altering statutes. Examined in this context, NEPA looks much better than its more unfriendly critics would like to admit. When sights are raised above the day-to-day efforts of government personnel to implement a policy for which few were prepared, the larger significance of NEPA can be seen. This significance is found in the idea that NEPA represents—in the policy commitment—and an effort to find a way to make the commitment operational. It is this significance of NEPA that has aroused interest in other countries, in states, provinces, and municipalities, and even in corporate enterprise.

Index

Abernathy, Rev. Ralph, 45
Academies of science: French, 29; Russian, 29; Ecole Politechnique, 30
Administrative Procedure Act (1946), 51, 54, 94
Advisory Council on Executive Reorganization, 36
Agency for International Development, 66
Air Pollution Control Association, 111
American Academy of Environmental Engineers, 111
American Academy of Sanitary Engineers. See American Academy of Environmental Engineers
American Association for the Advancement of Science, 15
American Enterprise Institute for Public Policy Research, 139
American Journal of Public Health, 40
American Medical Association, 40
American Society of Professional Ecologists, 111
Antarctica, 33; Antarctic Treaty of 1959, 34
Antienvironmentalism, 37, 65, 138–39, 146–48
Aspen Institute, 116
Association of Economic Poisons Control Officers. See Association of Pesticide Control Officers

Association of Pesticide Control Officers, 111
Association of State and Interstate Water Pollution Control Administrators, 111
Atlantic, The, 146
Atomic Energy Commission, 11, 35, 48, 58, 67

Bache, Alexander, 33
Bacon, Francis: dictum, 31, 123
Bandurski, Bruce L. (BLM), 134
Big Pine Reservoir, 86
Biosphere, 23; Conference, 44
Bonneville Dam, 41
Boundary Waters Treaty of 1909, 24, 86
Branscomb, Lewis M., 91–92
Bulletin of the Atomic Scientists, 102
Bureau of Land Management (BLM), 54, 55, 63, 74, 82, 84, 105, 119, 134, 135; integration of environmental impact assessment, 68, 70. *See also* California Desert Plan
Bureau of Outdoor Recreation (BOR), 56
Bureau of Reclamation, 8, 42, 55, 57, 81, 85–86

Calhoun, John B., 5